We offer two dedications,
one cosmic, one earthly:

to the HOLY SPIRIT
and
to DR. EDWIN SHNEIDMAN

Dying to Be Free

Dying to Be Free

A Healing Guide for Families after a Suicide

Beverly Cobain *and* Jean Larch

Hazelden
Center City, Minnesota 55012-0176
1-800-328-0094
1-651-213-4590 (Fax)
www.hazelden.org

Library of Congress Cataloging-in-Publication Data
Cobain, Bev, 1940–
Dying to be free : a healing guide for families after a suicide / Beverly Cobain and Jean Larch.
p. cm.
Includes bibliographical references and index.
ISBN-10: 1-59285-329-3
ISBN-13: 978-1-59285-329-8
1. Suicide—United States. 2. Adjustment (Psychology). 3. Bereavement—Psychological aspects. I. Larch, Jean, 1951– II. Title.

HV6548.U5C63 2006
155.9'37—dc22 2005052824

09 08 07 06 05 6 5 4 3 2 1

Cover design by David Spohn
Interior design and typesetting by Stanton Publication Services, Inc.

This book includes the authors' personal accounts of dealing with suicide, as well as others' true stories and photographs, all reprinted or adapted with permission. In some cases, names, dates, and circumstances have been changed to protect anonymity, but most individuals have requested that real names be used. The photographs on pages xi–xiii depict people who have died by suicide.

Contents

Acknowledgments

We wish to express our sincerest gratitude to

Dr. Edwin Shneidman, psychiatrist, researcher, author, and philosopher, who gave us the gift of his time, knowledge, and expertise;
Mark Larch, for his support, love, and prayers;
the hundreds of survivors of suicide who enlightened us with their experience;
the myriad survivors and attempters who courageously shared their pain;
our editor, Rebecca Post, and the staff at Hazelden for their hard work, and for believing in us;
all the contributors of photos and connection stories;
the staff of Macomb County Crisis Center in Chesterfield, Michigan, especially Jeni Koviak;
Tom and Ellen Paré for their editing skills;
Selene Wadhawan and Renée Doviak Bougenoy for their support and love;
author and friend Joel Rothschild for his encouragement and love;
Melissa Dawson;
Maggie Lother for her encouragement and cinnamon buns;
Brenda Reeves; and
Lisa Hurka-Covington.

No Resolve

So this is how you leave me
Bleeding where I stand
I've tried so hard to figure out
I've tried to understand
What could have been so goddamn painful
What it was that made you feel it had to end

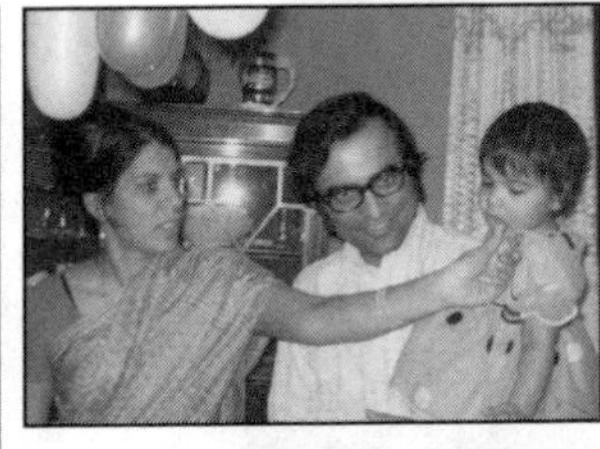

What was that final puzzle piece
You couldn't get to fit?
Did you take a minute to stop and think
How we would deal with it?
There'll be no answers to these questions
We've got to carry on and try to live

From top, left to right: Mary, Tyler, Alex, Dorcus and Jatinder, David

So goodbye I can't believe you're gone
So goodbye somehow I hope that you can
hear this song

Was there something
that I could have done
That might have changed
your mind?
If I told you I love you
and I need you here
Would you still be alive?

And though I know it's not my fault
I still carry all this guilt and shame inside

So goodbye I can't believe you're gone
So goodbye somehow I hope that you
can hear this song

From top, left to right: John, Joshua, Robert, Laura, Kurt, Kevin

To this song there is no ending
For this pain there's no resolve
Time won't cover up the wound
When you lose someone you love
If I could ask you one last thing
I guess that I would ask you why
I'd ask you why

So goodbye I can't believe you're gone
So goodbye somehow I hope that you can
hear this song

From top, left to right: Tony, Jason, Josh, Scott, Zachary, Mark

Music and lyrics copyright © 2003 by Dennis Liegghio; recorded and performed by the Student Driver Band, of which Dennis is a member. Reprinted with permission. Dennis was fourteen when his father, Mark Polance, died by suicide. Grief-stricken, he anesthetized himself with alcohol and drugs for years. Now in recovery, he expresses his soul in songs such as this.

Foreword

When I met with Bev Cobain and Jean Larch to discuss their forthcoming book, I knew that it was badly needed. As one who has lost a loved one to suicide, I saw that it could be an important healing tool for people like me.

Dying to Be Free is everything I hoped it would be and more, its insights cutting though the silence and stigma associated with this topic. Stories throughout the book leap from the pages to touch the soul. It speaks not only to "survivors of suicide" like me, but also to anyone who may have suicidal thoughts themselves, or who have attempted it, have lived through it, and are still battling agonizing pain.

We "survivors" need all the help we can get. Suicide changes the course of our lives forever. We need understanding and compassion, and if we are to survive and live well, we need education. We need to comprehend what could possibly have led to this devastating act.

I learned firsthand that suicide is a death with repercussions unlike any other. No words, no eloquent description, could ever convey the feelings that racked me while I held the cold, gray body of my beloved. Only another survivor knows the shock, rage, and agony that took me to my knees when I discovered his corpse. I heard my voice screaming,

"No, God, no!" I begged God to wake me from my nightmare. But my nightmare was real. Never have I felt so alone. I rocked and cried as I held the lifeless body of the best friend I have ever known.

My mind was consumed with *if only's.* If only I had come home a few hours earlier. If only I had seen some warning signs. If only he had told me how much he was suffering. That night my own suffering began as I unwillingly tried to imagine how I could live without this person whom I deeply loved.

That was ten years ago. Today, I wonder how my life might be different if this book had existed back then, but I, like you, can only move forward. You hold a means of moving forward in your hands right now. This book will answer a great many of your questions about suicide and explain the process that clouds the mind of the suicidal person. It will help you make some sense of what you thought was a totally senseless act.

I pray you will let the authors of this book take you by the hand, help you avoid the swamp of misinformation on this subject, and lead you to the truths that enlighten and make healing possible. If you have lost a loved one to suicide, or if you or someone you love has ever considered it, perhaps an angel or some Higher Power has placed this book in your hands. Please, take it home now and read it.

Joel Rothschild
June 2005
Los Angeles, California

Preface

In 1994, Kurt Cobain, twenty-seven-year-old front man for the band Nirvana, shot himself to death. It was a shot heard around the world, and it left an entire generation of young people devastated, reeling, and struggling to make sense of this tragic loss. Kurt's suicide left his family, friends, and fans feeling rejected, grief-stricken, guilty, and angry.

Why would a talented, wealthy young man with a loving family and a brilliant career already in progress end it all in one moment with a shotgun? Answering this profound question—why anyone might intentionally end his or her life—is one of the goals of this book. But the coauthors have two other goals as well. We want to help you, the reader, begin the journey of healing if you have experienced the suicide of a loved one. And we want to suggest some steps you might take to possibly prevent the suicide of yet another loved one—or even yourself in the future.

It is our hope that this book will offer you more knowledge about this human problem, and perhaps some insight into the dynamics of suicidal thinking that can lead to the act itself.

Much of the material in this book is born of our interviews with "survivors of suicide"—that is, the family and friends of the person who died—and with leading thinkers in the field. We have drawn on our combined forty years of working with, and learning from, suicidal individuals and survivors who have openly shared their innermost feelings and thoughts with us.

About us: Beverly Cobain, an author and psychiatric nurse, is a survivor of three family suicides, including that of her cousin Kurt Cobain. Since 1989, Jean Larch's "Understanding Suicide" workshop has helped hundreds of individuals gain a better understanding of the suicidal mind. As her workshop became established, it inspired our collaborative writing of this book. This has been a work of enthusiasm, love, and compassion. May it help you, the reader, to find what you need.

Beverly Cobain
Jean Larch

One

Every Seventeen Minutes

The telephone jars me awake the morning of April 8, 1994. I croak a "hello" into the phone. At first I don't recognize the voice that greets me: a quiet male voice, with an edge of excitement. "Is this Bev Cobain?" he asks, and identifies himself as a local newspaper reporter with whom I have spoken on previous occasions. I am distracted by the sun shining in my eyes and I want to go back to sleep. The reporter's next words change that.

"Bev, they just found a body dead of a shotgun blast in Kurt's house, but they're not sure who it is." He is speaking about my cousin Kurt Cobain, front man for the rock band Nirvana.

I'm stunned into silence, but suddenly awake. My mind searches for meaning in his words. Someone has discovered a body. Someone is dead in Kurt's house in Seattle. They don't know who it is. Then I remember something important.

"It can't be Kurt. He's in treatment in California."

The reporter adds a detail new to me. "Kurt abandoned the treatment center a few days ago. Bev, they think it's Kurt."

There is silence on the line. I can't breathe. Maybe it isn't

Kurt. Who could it be? My mind is buzzing with confusion. My eyes hurt. I don't get it. How can they not know whether it's Kurt? Everyone knows what Kurt looks like. I feel my heart jumping and thudding against my chest. My brain is trying to tell me something that my mind does not want to know. The message suddenly gets through and the shock of it brings me out of bed and drops me to my knees. They don't know whose body it is because there is no face!

Oh my God! Oh my God! Oh my God! Now I know it is Kurt, and I know he has killed himself. He has done the very thing I tried to warn his grandfather about. He is twenty-seven, the same age as my son Michael. Young, talented, beautiful, funny, sweet, smart. Gone. Sobbing, I hang up the phone.

I am devastated. I am afraid for his wife and child, his parents, siblings, relatives, and his friends. I am terrified for his fans. The possibility of copycat suicides is very real among the millions of kids and young adults who adore Kurt, look up to him, try to imitate him, and believe they are kindred spirits.

I am afraid for me. Afraid of the anger and of the guilt welling up within me. I pace back and forth in my bedroom, crying and talking aloud. I should have done more to save him. At some level I know this thought is ridiculous, even arrogant. Still, I am a psychiatric nurse, for God's sake! I knew he was in trouble. I saw his sadness and rage in his antics on television and in media articles, and I heard them in his lyrics. I knew he was at very high risk for suicide, that he was obsessed with guns and kept several in his house. I knew he was addicted to drugs. The two prior suicides in our family raised his risk significantly.

I had felt like an unwelcome intruder weeks earlier when I spoke to my uncle, Kurt's grandfather, about my fears for Kurt's life. He said he wasn't worried. Why didn't I insist he take me more seriously? Why was I afraid of frightening him? I felt helpless.

Now I remember the white T-shirt Kurt wore onstage and in photographs, the shirt on which he had written for all the world to see, "I hate myself and I want to die." Could his pain and risk for suicide have been made any clearer? Why hadn't I done more? Right now all I can do is cry.

Kurt Cobain's suicide was one of 31,000 reported annually in the United States. According to national suicide prevention organizations, a suicide occurs in this country every seventeen minutes. Sadly, in spite of prevention efforts by researchers, scientists, and other professionals, the rate is not falling. We now have suicidology—the study of suicide—and suicidologists, yet we still don't know what causes it, how to prevent it, or how to predict it. The statistics available today are based primarily on estimates and conjecture. There is no way to know what the real numbers are.

Nevertheless, several reliable organizations do track reported data and offer estimates. These include the American Association of Suicidology (AAS), American Foundation for Suicide Prevention (AFSP), the Centers for Disease Control and Prevention (CDC) and the National Center for Health Statistics (NCHS), the National Alliance for the

Mentally Ill (NAMI), Suicide Awareness Voices of Education (SAVE), the World Health Organization (WHO), and the Yellow Ribbon Suicide Prevention Program. More statistical data can be found at these groups' Web sites, listed at the back of this book.

If you are a "survivor of suicide"—and here this term means a person who has lost a loved one to suicide—you are not alone. A suicide occurs every seventeen minutes in the United States; eighty-eight each day, according to AAS estimates.[1] Left in their wake are about forty new survivors each hour; almost a thousand each day. There are an astounding ten million survivors living today.[2]

Four times as many males as females complete suicide, although female attempts outnumber male attempts three to one. Firearms are used in about 60 percent of cases.[3] Each year, nearly twice as many Americans die by their own hand as by homicide.[4] In 2000, suicide accounted for almost half of all violent deaths worldwide.[5]

Young people are a significant part of this critical public health issue. About every two hours a young American dies by suicide; it is the second most frequent cause of death for college students, the third most frequent for youth fifteen to twenty.[6] And even among children ten to fourteen, the rate has more than doubled since 1990; in 2001 there were 272 known suicides in this age group.[7]

And reported data can only tell part of the story. The actual magnitude of this problem is utterly unknown; the numbers may conceivably be as high as double those estimated above.

"Whenever figures on suicide are presented or discussed, there are always those who question their reliability, insisting that in many places, and due to several factors, suicides are hidden and that the real figures must be much higher. We acknowledge this point and believe it reinforces the gravity of the problem of suicide."[8]

—World Health Organization 1999 Report

Nor does suicide respect boundaries. No matter what a person's social or economic status, religion, education, IQ, race, gender, or age, suicide strikes within them all. And prevention is problematic. Despite what experts tell us about risk factors, warning signs are rarely given any significance before the tragedy occurs, leaving families and friends shocked and incapacitated, workmates and communities stunned. In addition, if it was a child or adolescent, entire school student bodies are left struggling with anxiety, confusion, sadness, and fear.

Uncertain Statistics

Several factors account for the unreliability of these estimates, including questionable intent and underreporting.

When the intent of the person who died is unclear, the manner of death is not easily determined. Circumstances may be ambiguous, especially in cases of overdose or self-poisoning because they occur so often and in uncertain contexts. Unless the person has left a note—fewer than one in four do—or is known to have been depressed and/or suicidal, self-poisoning may seem like a natural death and not be drawn to a coroner's attention. Other suicides might appear accidental, such as driving a car into a tree (autocide), insulin overdoses, some firearm deaths, "falls" from high places, and some drownings.

Thirteen-year-old Ashley, after a family argument, suddenly opened the back door of their moving vehicle and rolled out onto the highway. Her father stopped the car and ran back to where his daughter lay unconscious. While the weeping father held her head in his lap, Ashley died. Although at first Ashley's death was recorded as a suicide, her family did not believe her jump from the car was a suicide attempt. They were able to have the manner of death on the death certificate changed to "accidental," since her intent remained questionable.

We believe, along with many experts, that reported cases tell only a small part of the story, and that the actual number of U.S. suicides over the past twenty years may be close to *one million.*

Psychiatrist and author Edwin Shneidman noted in 2004, "In the United States, we are sure that accurate statistics are nonexistent. Among the experts there remains much confusion and difference of interpretation about how to classify deaths. What may be considered a suicide in one locality is often reported as an accident in another."[9]

A related factor is stigma. Although families may know a loved one killed himself, they often vehemently deny it to avoid public scorn and scrutiny. They report a different cause of death; insulin and other overdoses are common examples. One survivor, Nina, found her husband dead of a shotgun blast to his head, but she never told anyone but the children what had actually happened. "I could never have let our friends know he killed himself," she said. "I told everyone it was a heart attack."

Prior Attempts: The Strongest Predictor for Suicide

After she was cleared by the hospital emergency room, fifteen-year-old Susan was admitted to the mental health unit following a suicide attempt by drug overdose. She was accompanied by her distraught parents, who adamantly claimed that their daughter had never done anything like this before, nor could they think of a reason she would "try something so crazy now." After her parents left, Susan disclosed that she had taken a handful of pills on three prior occasions, but had unexpectedly awakened in the morning, ashamed to tell anyone, and feeling more helpless than ever.

Susan's story is an all too common one, and again, numbers can only suggest the gravity of the problem. For the year 2001, the AAS estimated 750,000 suicide attempts—that is, more than 2,000 a day, 85 each hour. Experts tell us that a total of some five million Americans have tried to kill themselves at some time. But the problem is much larger than that. For each adult suicide completed, at least 25 attempts are made; for adolescents, as many as 200.[10] Of the 31,000 completed suicides per year, about 26,000 are adults, 5,000 are youth. Therefore, we can count attempts at some 650,000 for adults and a million for youth annually in the United States—astounding and unacceptable numbers.

Unfortunately, it is an enormous global problem as well. In 2000 the World Health Organization estimated a million suicides annually worldwide, with attempts exceeding them tenfold, perhaps twentyfold. What does this mean? One death by suicide on our planet every forty seconds, and one attempt every three seconds.[11]

Very often, following a suicide, families learn of at least one prior attempt. Many people who survive an attempt never tell anyone. Others may swear a friend to secrecy. These secrets make it impossible to obtain accurate figures—but prior attempts continue to be the strongest predictor for suicide.

"I returned from work that evening to find my daughter hanging in the garage," said Michael, a survivor father. "After the funeral I set out to find out why she had wanted to die. I was talking to one of her friends, who then broke down in sobs and told me Brenda had tried to hang herself the week before, but the belt had broken. She told this friend but swore her to secrecy."

Today, in a typical American high school, one-third of students say they know of someone who had attempted suicide but didn't die. With some 800,000 young people doing so each year, the gravity of this issue is being greatly underestimated. Notably, suicide attempts are not tracked in the United States, and attempts not requiring medical attention are not likely to be reported.

According to various media sources, Kurt Cobain was

found near death in a hotel room in Rome on the first day of March 1994. It was reported as an accidental overdose and therefore not a suicide attempt. Kurt shot himself thirty-seven days later. When a person can no longer tolerate the intense psychological pain, when he reaches the point where death seems the only way out, without some kind of meaningful intervention it is only a matter of time until the suicide.

Nathan
1984–1997

Leah, a survivor, tells about her brother Nathan.

I was the one who found Nathan dead of carbon monoxide poisoning in the garage. I tried to wake him up, and when I couldn't, I felt my heart die.

The next twenty-four hours were hell. I cried until I couldn't cry anymore. I was so hysterical that the cops had to have someone watch me because they thought I might kill myself.

Nathan never wrote a note, but he had written on the garage door, "House of pain."

My mom thought Nathan was murdered, and she tried to kill herself twice. She was in a psychiatric ward for two weeks and then went into a horrible depression. I couldn't be around my mother because all she was doing was crying and saying how she wanted to die.

I don't feel my needs were ever met. I needed a father, but he died when I was twelve. I needed my grandmother, and she died the following year. My grandfather died a year later; then, when I was fifteen, my little brother killed himself. Everyone I loved was dying.

I needed my mother, but we never got along. Four months before Nathan killed himself, my mom started hitting me, and I beat her up in front of Nathan. I'm not proud of that, and I was made to go live with my godparents.

I didn't even know what suicide was until Nathan killed himself. After I learned a little more about killing yourself, I recognized some signs. For example, the last week I saw my brother alive he was giving away his toys. He asked me if our father, who had passed away, was in heaven. I so wish I had known he was hurting inside.

For a while after the suicide, I tried to stay strong for everyone. I started working and hanging out with my friends, and I did everything I could to keep myself busy so I wouldn't miss my little brother . . . so I wouldn't think about his death and the fact that I would never see him again.

Anyone suffering the loss of a loved one by suicide should definitely talk to someone. They should never keep the pain inside, because you only hurt more. The pain is still buried deep inside. You should go to therapy, talk to someone, whether it be a friend or family member. Get all that grief out of there. I called the local suicide prevention hotline and talked to a counselor who listened to me and who was interested in what I had to say.

What unimaginable horror causes a thirteen-year-old boy to believe he will be better off dead? Suicide is a complicated issue, but some possible answers will be revealed as we explore the suicidal mind.

Two

The Suicidal Mind

Survivors know that even the most promising life may end in suicide. Jeff's story illustrates how dangerously and quickly one's thinking can become constricted and narrowed. This talented young man became so overwhelmed with inner turmoil that he saw no other solution to his pain. His story is retold here with details provided by his mother, Diane.

Jeff
1969–1989

Jeff was an intelligent boy who taught himself to read at age four. Though his parents were divorced when he was very young, outwardly he seemed to thrive. As a teen, he enjoyed writing and became editor of his high school paper. He was one of one hundred juniors in Washington state high schools to be selected for the first Governor's School for Citizen Leadership, a month-long program focusing on local, state, national, and international issues. Jeff performed in plays for the annual playwrights' forum at the local civic theater. In his senior year, a play Jeff wrote was performed, and he won a five-state regional award for his writing. He played recreational and varsity soccer and began coaching boys aged thirteen and fourteen, continuing until a month before he died three years later.

In November 1989, when he was twenty, Jeff began having problems. He had moved out of his mother's home. He had a girlfriend who was disliked by his friends. He had trouble keeping food down, and he withdrew from friends and family. His girlfriend got into trouble with the law and went to jail. Jeff said he felt his life was falling apart. His friends later recalled that when they did see him, Jeff joked about death. They believed he was only joking.

On November 29, Jeff didn't go to work, and no one was able to reach him by phone. The following day, a friend went to his house to check on him. He found Jeff in the garage, dead of carbon monoxide poisoning.

A short story Jeff had written two years before his suicide was found among his things. It was about an angel who talked a young man out of jumping from a bridge. In the story, the main character was experiencing the same problems and turmoil that Jeff had gone through before his suicide.

The Growth of "Psychache"

When life becomes difficult, when stresses intensify and situations change, some people become overwhelmed with turmoil. They begin to back away from their lives. They keep the growing hurt to themselves until it becomes so profound that they fear it will never go away. Still, they may deny any problems if others ask. What happens when mental and psychological distress becomes crushing and impossible to bear?

Mental distress

Everyone experiences some level of mental distress each day. Things go wrong, plans backfire, people are let go from jobs, friends disagree, relationships change, tests are failed, games are lost, dinners are burned—such mishaps occur in all of our lives. Most people are able to talk about the hurt or anger, cry, yell, confront, discuss—whatever they are in the habit of doing to feel better during a bad day.

Unfortunately, not everyone is capable of dealing effectively with such problems. Many individuals hold negative beliefs about themselves that keep them from managing their lives successfully. A woman seen by others as pretty, talented, and self-assured may perceive herself as homely, stupid, and incompetent. Who that person is and will become is determined not by how others see her, or even by how she really is, but by her own perceptions of herself. Some people don't have the life experience to handle a great deal of turmoil, and they look to supportive others to help. Others have learned to endure problems by ignoring them or running from them. Some turn to counterproductive methods, such as numbing pain through abuse of alcohol, food, and/or drugs.

Unmet needs

Every human being has certain basic physical needs. Air, water, food, shelter, and a favorable temperature are absolutely necessary to sustain life. We also have basic psychological needs. We may not be consciously aware of them, but if they go unsatisfied, inner turmoil can result. Edwin

Shneidman, psychiatrist, author, researcher, and philosopher, formulated these basic needs, adapted here as the following:

1. The need for love, nurturing relationships, and feeling connected
2. The need for control over feelings, life, and environment
3. The need for a positive self-image and self-worth
4. The need to avoid humiliation, embarrassment, and shame
5. The need to question and understand[1]

Most of us grow to adulthood with some of these basic psychological needs unmet. As our lives progress, many of us learn to get most of our needs met in appropriate ways. Others of us repeat the same mistakes over and over in our quest to feel fulfilled, and so have varying degrees of mental distress for much of our lives.

What is psychache?

Mental distress is experienced as pain in the mind. The term for this kind of pain, as coined by Shneidman, is *psychache*. *Psych* refers to the mind, and *ache* refers to the anguish, hurt, and misery that the person is experiencing. The word, therefore, means pain in the mind, as described by Shneidman in his book *The Suicidal Mind*.[2]

We must all face turmoil at times, and everyone experiences episodes of psychache throughout their lives. Ordinarily, people handle them as they occur. But when turmoil is not appropriately addressed, psychache may build until it becomes intolerable. At these heightened levels, some people begin to have the idea of death as the *only* way to end their pain. When heightened psychache and this idea occur together, suicide is often the result. Shneidman's groundbreaking work tells us that it is possible to have psychache without suicide, but there is no suicide without psychache. The accompanying diagram shows how these factors can increase risk.

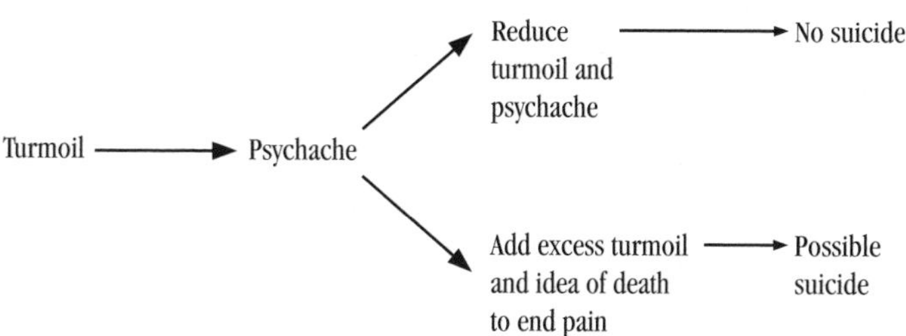

These two factors, together, can lead to suicide:

- intolerable mental pain (psychache), with
- the idea of death to escape it[3]

The relationship of mind and brain

Thoughts exist in the mind. The mind is a complex and creative entity, existing outside the body, but greatly influencing the functions of the brain. The brain makes it possible for us to have a mind. No brain, no mind. The brain is necessary for the mind to exist and to think. But thoughts, beliefs, hopes, and dreams—as well as fantasies, imaginings, dramas, and ideas—are found not in the brain but within the mind.

The work of the brain is to keep the body healthy and functioning normally, *but the brain also functions as a servant to the mind.* What the mind believes (thinks to be true), the brain will attempt to make happen. Thoughts in the mind are the beginning of almost everything. Other than in the natural world, everything we see, feel, or do was first a thought in someone's mind, from the classic novels to giant skyscrapers, the use of fire, and the Great Wall of China. The mind is very powerful, and it is important to mind your thoughts.

Psychiatric disorders are physical dysfunctions of the brain and can often be treated with medications. Suicide, on the other hand, is best addressed through the treatment of human emotions; it is an issue of the mind. The solution to suicide lies in reducing psychache.

Some people reduce their own psychache by using methods they know or have learned: meditating; talking with a friend, therapist, or teacher; having a massage; reading self-help books; joining a group of like-minded people; making a decision that eliminates a problem; or changing certain behaviors. Friends or family members may unwittingly say or do something to ease the psychache for a time: they visit, suggest an outing, offer help with a problem, express compassion and caring. Showing concern can make all the difference: listen to what is going on with the person and be available for frank discussions whenever possible. Anyone can ask the question, "Where do you hurt the most right now? What will make you feel better?" However, many sufferers will not speak of their pain and turmoil, feeling that it is too personal or that they will be judged harshly. And as it intensifies, they may be even less willing to speak of it.

Talk therapy with a competent therapist or religious/spiritual advisor is one way to reduce psychache. More approaches will be discussed in later chapters.

A woman named Martha sits with enough pills to kill herself. When asked what is propelling her toward suicide, she cites a series of losses: Her husband has died recently of a heart attack. She has lost her home, her car has broken down, and she has just learned she has a brain tumor. When asked which of her losses is most distressing, Martha replies that it is the absence of her husband, whom she relied upon for everything. Along with talk therapy once a week, she decides to join a grief support group. To reduce her heightened psychache more immediately, she thinks of writing a letter to her dead husband, expressing her pain on paper. She plans to leave the letter at the cemetery, where she frequently goes to find comfort. For now, Martha's psychache has lessened, and she's open to options other than suicide.

Three

The Fatal Journey

All of us experience some degree of psychache at times during our lives. Emotional distress is part of living. Why are some individuals able to live with it for long periods of time without ever considering suicide? Why do some people kill themselves while others don't? When psychache intensifies, it, along with the idea of death as the only way to escape it, becomes the driving force behind suicide. Those who kill themselves do not want to die. They are, however, willing to die when they see no other solution to their pain.

The circumstances leading to suicide are different for each person, but some similarities may be seen in their thought patterns. The suicidal journey begins with inner turmoil: unresolved problems and unmet emotional needs leading to heightened psychache. The person obsesses over what is wrong in his life. His problems play over and over in his mind, and his attempt to cope with them depletes his energy and further twists his perceptions. His thinking narrows so that he can perceive no way out. He begins the slide into despair.

A secret dialogue begins inside his mind. A part of him wishes to live while another part wants to die, and he may be making plans for the future at the same time he is considering suicide. This ambivalence is characteristic of the suicidal mind. He may be open to help from supportive others as he continues to search for reasons to stay alive, but he will probably not ask for help verbally. He may give clues, some vague, some more direct, though it is usually only in retrospect that any significance is applied to them. His inability to communicate feelings to others intensifies his helplessness and confusion, and he begins to formulate a plan for suicide.

The Tunnel

A kind of tunnel vision develops when suicide is viewed as the *only* solution to ending one's pain. Although he is loved by family and friends, this is no longer enough to sustain him. The love he has for family and others has neither changed nor been forgotten, but he cannot concentrate on anything but his own pain. Once he enters the tunnel, those who love him are outside his view. He has emotionally detached from everyone; his sense of isolation increases. Should something occur to ease his psychache before he enters the tunnel, he may abandon the idea of suicide for the moment. He may move toward the tunnel many times over the next hours, months, or even years. When the psychache heightens to an unbearable level, when he perceives death as the only solution to his pain—and if nothing happens to reduce that pain—he may enter the tunnel.

Inside the tunnel, ambivalence decreases as the suicidal person is unwilling to endure further pain. As he moves deeper into the tunnel, ironically, his outward symptoms may improve. The person may stop treatments such as counseling or medication, and loved ones may see this as a sign of progress, of feeling better. Meanwhile, however, his negative thoughts about himself intensify. In his mind, he is neither lovable nor worthy of rescue. He believes death is the only way out: his world is unmanageable, and no one and nothing can help him anymore. The suicidal mind judges that he has tried everything to rid himself of his intolerable pain, and no option remains except death. This judgment has nothing to do with reality, but he cannot recognize this. Internal resources such as love for others, self-worth, positive thinking, hope, and faith, can no longer be accessed. He devises the plan for escape. He will end the pain by killing it.

Masters of deception

The impaired thoughts of the suicidal mind are now separated from the emotions. Thinking becomes calm, methodical, and focused on death. At this stage, the person knows precisely how, when, and where he will kill himself. He is in control of his life and destiny for the first time. He is not afraid of dying; he is more afraid of living. He is so relieved that his struggle will soon be over that he may suddenly appear happy, even euphoric. Friends and family are now convinced they have worried for nothing.

> *"I was so sly about my suicide attempts that no one knew of my plans."*
>
> —Lee, suicide survivor and attempter

Although the person appears to be back to normal, he secretly prepares to act on his plan. He believes he is a burden to those he cares about, and that they will be better off without him. Mechanically, void of feelings, he may write a note, visit family and friends, make a will, return borrowed items, give personal possessions away, and obtain the means to end his life. He can end his pain at any moment. It is his secret. He will tell no one of his plan. He has become a master of deception and is standing at the edge of his life.

Many survivors report a strange or empty look in the person's eyes in the hours before the suicide. The look is often fleeting, but may last longer.

At the time of the suicide, his mind is quiet. No more emotional agony. The war is over. There is no fear, only a deep inner peace. Now, by whatever means he has devised, he ends his suffering. The suffering of his loved ones begins.

On the Edge

The slide toward the tunnel is not always a gradual one. For some people, psychache comes and goes abruptly, often accompanied by suicidal thoughts. A person may wake up to find the tunnel suddenly gaping near at hand. Beverly Cobain shares the following true account of her own suicidal journey, which took place in its entirety within just twelve hours.

I awakened slowly that Sunday morning. As I lay there, eyes closed, I became increasingly aware of a sense of loss and anxiety. Dread and despair brought me fully awake. I felt as though some evil alien thing had invaded my body as I slept. It would be impossible to sink back into the peace of unconsciousness now. I hadn't felt like this for more than three years. The pain was back.

For years I suffered from bouts of insomnia lasting weeks at a time. Sudden attacks of fear over my seemingly imminent death had terrified me from age thirteen. Once, in the midst of a recurrence of these symptoms, a friend drove me to a supermarket and I sat in his car sobbing. I couldn't get out of the car. I felt that someone had pulled plugs from the bottoms of my feet, and all of my life force was draining out.

Eventually I found a therapist who worked with me weekly for four years to boost my feelings of self-worth and confidence. One of the many medical doctors I had seen over the years had prescribed tranquilizers for my "neuroses." Another ran lung function tests but could determine no physical reason for a breathing problem that was terrifying me. My symptoms were all in my mind, said another doctor, making a circle beside his ear with one finger. Other doctors diagnosed me as frigid, alcoholic, and a hypochondriac. I was ashamed to go to doctors anymore.

Not one of them, over a twenty-year period, suggested I might be depressed. Not one medical doctor asked any of the right questions or recognized my symptoms, which were classic for post-traumatic stress disorder (PTSD) and major depression. Not one referred me for a mental health evaluation or to a psychiatrist.

I hoped the anguish I was experiencing was not all "in my head," and I knew I couldn't go on this way. I had to have relief. Thankfully, a concerned friend recommended I meet her psychiatrist. He was like a magician. The questions he asked addressed exactly what I had been struggling with for most of my life. He recognized major depression and PTSD within the first appointment. My anxiety was treated and resolved almost immediately, and we tried various antidepressants until we found one that helped me. Within a few weeks, the other symptoms disappeared, my energy returned, and I could sleep and eat and laugh. I was the real me again.

Now, three years later, I tried to act as if everything was the same as it had been the day before. I showered, went downstairs, made coffee. I sat in my beautiful living room looking out over a lovely lake and sipped sweet coffee while absolute hopelessness slid over me like a shroud, and I cried. I couldn't bear to go through all the pain again. No more suffering. I was barely surprised when I heard myself say aloud: *"If I still feel this bad at seven o'clock tonight, I'm going to shoot myself."* I knew I meant it.

I remember little of the rest of that day. Perhaps the pain was too great. I do remember wishing in the back of my mind that someone would call or drop by, but no one did. I don't know what I thought about. I just watched the clock.

My next memory is of climbing the stairs back to my bedroom at six o'clock that evening. I felt numb, more like a robot than a living being. I took my loaded pistol from the nightstand drawer, sat on the edge of my bed, and laid it beside me. Curiously, I placed the phone on the bed beside the gun. I believe I was still hoping someone would call. No one did. Every few minutes I checked to see if the gun was loaded. It was fully loaded with hollow-point rounds. I replaced the gun beside me on the bed and watched the clock.

At six forty-five, I began looking around my bedroom as if seeing it for the first time. It was a nice room, large, with white walls. The carpet and window shades were pale silver. I studied the walls and carpet carefully. I began to realize that blood would really make a mess. As my eyes roamed around the room, I "saw" blood in a specific place near the top of the stairs. My mind tried to make sense of "seeing" blood in that certain spot. I could see that the blood wouldn't be where I envisioned it unless I moved to a different part of the room. If I shot myself sitting on the bed, the blood would not spill where I "saw" it. This confused me.

I must emphasize a crucial point: at no time during that day or evening did I think about my family, my children, my friends, my therapist, or how any of them might react to my death. It was not that I didn't love or care about all of them. They just weren't part of my state of mind. I was totally hopeless and focused on the only way I could imagine to free myself from unbearable emotional pain.

The clock clicked onto seven o'clock. I noticed it was growing darker outside and turned on the bedside lamp. It was time. I do not remember making a decision; my arm simply reached out for the gun, and when I looked at my hand again, it held the telephone. Whether by divine intervention or my own will, I dialed the number of a close friend. I've no idea what I would have done had she not answered her telephone, but she did, and I heard my expressionless voice say, "I'm sitting on my bed with my gun and I think I'm going to kill myself." There was silence for a few moments. When she spoke again, I heard fear in her voice. She asked if she could call my therapist—who was also her own—and have her call me right back. I said, "She'd better hurry." I hung up and waited a minute or two. Just as I picked up the gun, the phone rang. It was Kay, my therapist, speaking in her calm, serene manner. To the best of my memory, the following is the dialogue that ensued.

Kay: "Bev? This is Kay. Where is the gun now?"

Me: "Beside me."

Kay: "I'm going to stay on the line while you unload the gun. Will you do that, please?"

Me: "Yes, just a moment." I removed all the rounds from the gun and laid them on the bed. "Okay."

Kay: "The gun is unloaded?"

Me: "Yes." Now I was crying.

Kay: "I'm going to stay on the line and wait while you take the empty gun to your car and lock it in the trunk. Okay?"

Me: "Okay, be right back." Robotlike, I did as she asked and returned to the phone.

Kay: "I would like you to come to my house now. Do you think you can drive safely?"

Me: "Mmm hmm."

Kay: "Come right this minute, okay? Don't stop to do anything. Just drive to my house now. Will you be okay until then?"

Me: "I think so."

Kay: "Please promise you won't do anything to yourself until we've talked."

Me: "I promise."

Kay: "I'll see you in about twenty-five minutes, then?"

Me: "Yes."

I put the phone down. Sobbing but greatly relieved, I locked the house and left. Nearly unable to see through my tears, I drove slowly to Kay's house. She was waiting at the door with a serious look on her face, but I knew her as a compassionate and kind person. Together we retrieved the empty gun from the trunk and went inside. Upstairs the guest room lamp was on, and a pair of flannel pajamas lay on the bed. The room was cozy and warm. We sat on the bed and I cried while she held me as a mother would hold a cherished child. I don't remember one thing we talked about. Later, her husband brought up hot chocolate and warm cookies, and it was in the wee morning hours that I finally slept.

When I awoke the next morning, no trace remained of the despair I had felt the day before. I was calm and relaxed. No hopelessness. No suicidal feelings. It was as if I had awakened from a nightmare. I was happy and grateful to be alive. The only negative feeling I had was shame that I had been responsible for so much drama.

I have never shared this experience in detail with any but my closest friends until now. Perhaps my story illustrates how a suicide can be impossible to predict. I have thought often about my two sons, whom I love dearly, and who would have been shocked and devastated. I can't explain why I woke up one morning and wanted to die. I was active and productive, working as a psychiatric nurse. It was within a year of Kurt's death, and I had been traveling the country, speaking to communities about youth suicide prevention. I was writing my first book.

Yes, I had had suicidal thoughts before, but I had never come so close to it. I was being treated for depression, but despite three years of antidepressant medication and four years of talk therapy, the urge to kill myself had suddenly surfaced. I believe it was divine intervention that saved me. Thank goodness for Kay, who provided the compassion and support I didn't even realize I needed.

I now think of this experience as a gift. When I address suicidal individuals and survivors, I relate on a personal level to their pain and suffering. I know the despair and hopelessness that precede suicide.

Common Characteristics

Suicide is a complicated issue. There is no way to determine exactly who is at risk and, therefore, no reliable means of prevention. There is no single common denominator in suicidal behavior, nor any one personality type that is predisposed to it. However, there are some common characteristics among people who die by suicide, as determined by "psychological autopsy"—interviews with friends, family, workmates, and others close to them. In this way, interviewers have noted some commonalities in the personality, attitudes, circumstances, coping methods, and social manners of many suicidal people.[1]

Because survivors usually feel they should or could have prevented the tragedy—or may even have caused it—learning about these commonalities can free them from those unrealistic ideas. They come to understand that the suicide was the responsibility of the deceased person, and not of those left behind. Let's look at some of these common traits and circumstances, with the awareness that they are not unique to suicidal people.

Perfectionism. Perfectionists have unrealistically high expectations of self and others. They avoid tasks they don't think they can do perfectly and become frustrated when they don't meet their own standards. They do high-quality work, but they may have relationship problems because they require perfection of others.

High achievement. They set high goals and always push

themselves to do better. They may be emotionally unsatisfied and believe they will never make it, no matter how hard they try.

Fear of failure. They may fear they will fail and be criticized. They may be unwilling to take risks. They may believe that success pleases others and failure causes people not to like them. They may not understand the value of learning from failure, and new experiences may be traumatic for them. Criticism can be devastating. They think they must please others to be "good" or "worthy."

Low self-esteem. They may feel worthless, useless, or burdensome to everyone. They may believe they are powerless to make things right, that the world would be a better place without them. They may fear others will find out how inadequate they are. Their despair leads to hopelessness.

Hopelessness. They may think they have tried all options, and life will never be better. They feel nothing and no one can help them, and nothing gives them joy.

Childhood trauma. They may have had a trauma at birth or at a young age. They may have had a significant loss due to divorce, death, illness, or other difficulty. They may have unresolved emotional conflicts or unmet needs, compounded by poor coping skills.

Communication problems. They may have difficulty communicating negative feelings, especially anger. They may tend to hold anger in until it explodes, pushing others away. They may feel isolated and believe others hold a low opinion of them.

Prior suicide attempt. This is the single strongest predictor of suicide. These past attempts are often not discovered by the family until after death. Attempts may be rehearsals for actual suicide.

Family history of suicide. Suicide itself is not hereditary. But if a relative has died by suicide, this can be seen as giving permission for other family members to attempt suicide. Some may believe they can join the person they lost.

Effect of father figure. The expectations of a father figure are perceived as impossible to meet—or that figure may be absent through death, illness, divorce, military career, or substance use.

Talent or high intelligence. Gifted people may feel pressured by others' high expectations. They often feel different and withdraw within themselves.

Tendency to question life's meaning. They may search for their purpose on earth or may be obsessed with whether God or another Higher Power exists.

Remember, everyone has some of these characteristics, but most people never consider suicide.

"She was the last person I would ever have expected to kill herself!" This remark is commonly heard following a suicide. There is a good reason for this. Most people have a false image of what a suicidal person should look and act like. They believe such a person must be suffering from clinical depression, appear lonely, sad, and isolated. There also exists the belief that only "losers" or "bad" or "crazy" people kill themselves; or only cowardly and selfish people. Bev Cobain recalled, "As I listened to an older man singing and playing his guitar one evening, I jokingly asked him to play something by Nirvana. He quickly turned to me with the stunning comment, 'I don't play music written by losers!'"

Indeed, prevention efforts would be more successful if suicidal individuals were as easily identified as these misconceptions would suggest.

In her "Understanding Suicide" workshops, which Jean Larch has conducted for the past fifteen years, she asks survivors what adjectives best describe their loved ones. They consistently report most of the following traits:

- loving
- funny
- carefree
- creative
- artistic
- outdoor type
- successful
- loved life
- caring
- giving
- active

Of course, many people have these traits and never take their lives, and not every suicidal person can be described with all these adjectives. Still, these are traits consistently seen by loved ones and, notably, these traits may mask the sufferer's pain. The suicidal individual is most often an ordinary person who may be a perfectionist, who may be a high achiever, and who fears failure. He has poor coping patterns, low self-esteem, and suppressed anger. But because these attributes are also present in nonsuicidal people, prevention is especially difficult.

No one wants to believe that someone they love or care for, someone who appears to have much to live for, bears the seeds of self-destruction. Yet for thousands of years, suicide has been the final choice for many people who have silently battled traumatizing pain. When those of us left in the aftermath inherit that pain, we can begin to understand and grieve for those precious lives—lives we would have done anything to save if only we had known their suffering.

Four

Survivors of Suicide

At the moment an individual ends his life, he ends his pain. In that very same moment, the suffering of those left behind begins. Suicide is a sudden and violent act. Even if it appears peaceful, those left behind feel traumatized and often ambushed. Even when a person has threatened it for months or years, or even attempted it, the reality of the actual death leaves survivors stricken with shock and disbelief.

Suicide alters the lives of survivors in an instant. The irreversible loss of a beloved person does not simply leave an empty hole in the life of the survivor. The body craves his presence, the mind is desperate to comprehend his absence, and the spirit yearns for relief of the loneliness. Survivors experience virtually the same psychache felt by the loved ones who took their own lives.

Marsha, a survivor mother, recounted the morning her son died. "I was just going to take a shower when I realized I couldn't hear Mac's music, the usual signal that he was up and getting ready for school. I rapped on his bedroom door, and when I didn't get a response, I looked inside, expecting to see him still asleep. My precious fourteen-year-old son had hanged himself from the top bunk bed. I thought I would never stop screaming."

Survivors may be terrified to the edge of sanity, incapacitated by shock and horror. Their wounds are not of the flesh, but of the mind and spirit. Engulfed by grief, they necessarily live moment by moment, putting one foot before the other, breathing in and breathing out. They feel disconnected from reality. Their world has suddenly become one of shattered dreams, endless nights, and inconsolable pain. They feel isolated, ashamed, guilty, angry, and totally in the dark about how to get through the next hour, day, week, month. They wonder if living is even possible without their loved one.

"I believed my life was over," said LaRita, a survivor mother. "Oh, I never doubted that my existence would and must continue, but I saw the rest of my life as pain-filled days stretching endlessly into years . . . to be endured without peace or hope of happiness."

> *"I was cooking dinner that night when the phone rang. I thought it was probably my husband, Ted, calling from the car to tell me he was stuck in traffic. I was totally unprepared for what happened when I answered the phone. First I heard Ted's voice say, 'Goodbye.' Then I heard the gunshot."*
>
> —Lila, survivor wife

Linda, another survivor mother, remembers similar feelings. "Two nights after our nineteen-year-old son died by suicide, my husband and I collapsed into bed," she said. "We were like two zombies lying there in terrible pain, sharing the same feelings of being simply overwhelmed with horror. Neither of us could sleep, and eventually my husband sighed, and then one of us asked, 'Do we want to live?' Finally we agreed that we did, that we had to, and that it would be incredibly hard. We held each other the rest of the night. Over the years, when sad things have happened, I know we've both remembered that night and that pledge, and it's helped us to go on."

As survivors begin to resume necessary activities, life virtually starts over for them. Each task is for the first time since the suicide. The first time to prepare a meal, pay a bill, take out the garbage, feed the dog. Daily chores are done on autopilot, or forgotten, or deemed unimportant. The body is exhausted. Thoughts spin, impossible to grasp. The mind tries desperately to make sense of what is happening. Nothing seems to matter anymore. Choosing which clothing to put on in the morning seems an insurmountable task. Survivors find themselves hurled into the complex maze of grief.

Survivor Grief Reactions

Grief is a natural and necessary reaction to a loss—and it is a process. After a suicide, the human mind is unable to fully take in the enormity of it: how it could have happened, why they didn't see it coming, what they could have done to stop it, what they should or shouldn't have said or done, how to live with the loss. Their reactions and emotions range widely as they slowly absorb what has happened, find appropriate support, and begin the process of reinventing their lives. It can take time. "How can the world just go on . . . shopping, driving, laughing?" wondered Sharon, a survivor mother. "Don't they know my son is dead?"

Denise, a survivor sister, recalled, "On the night my brother, Robert, killed himself, I was away at college. My brother and I were very close, and when my fiancé told me of his suicide, I knew it couldn't be my brother. I was sure there was a mistake, and wanted to go home immediately and see for myself. When I realized it was true, I was totally horrified, and immediately burdened with heavy, heavy guilt. He was my best friend. How could it be that I hadn't known how much he was hurting?"

The closer the survivors were, emotionally, to the special person, the longer, more painful, and intense will be their grief. Grief is not an event; grief is a process. Survivors who are prematurely urged by well-meaning individuals to "move on" need to know the importance of grieving on their *own* schedules. To attempt to grieve according to another's wishes causes increased pain and confusion.

Common reactions

As people move through grief, they may experience these reactions in varying intensities at various times. Discussed in more detail in the pages following, these reactions include

- Shock/Denial. Survivors may be unable to believe the loved one is gone, or that it was suicide.
- Anxiety/Panic. They have feelings of helplessness and loss of control.
- Anger/Blame. Often they have misplaced anger toward God, others, or self.
- Resistance/Avoidance. They may hide behind behaviors that postpone dealing with grief, such as travel, overworking, substance abuse, and so on.
- Immobility/Withdrawal. They may feel disoriented, disorganized, and unable to function normally.
- Transition. They begin to renew interests in self, others, and life in general.

Grief reactions do not follow a chronological path. Survivors may move back and forth among them over time, addressing various issues. There are no rules to follow in grieving, no time frames, no set pattern, no right or wrong way.

Shock/Denial

At first, survivors find it difficult to believe the death has actually happened. Shock and denial can paralyze survivors as they try to grasp the unthinkable. They are sometimes unwilling to believe the death was self-inflicted. This reaction may include feelings of numbness, serving to delay the feelings of horror. "I truly believed my daughter's death was an accident," said Andrea, a survivor mother. "How could someone so young even think of killing herself? It wasn't until her friends admitted that she had been talking about suicide that I realized she really had meant to die."

Anxiety/Panic

Anxiety results when one fears that something bad will happen in the future. Anxiety occurs in the mind. The brain receives the message and responds to the mind's fear by alerting the body that it must prepare for "fight or flight." Symptoms may include

- sweating
- heart palpitations
- chest pain
- tremors
- crying
- air hunger (feeling a scarcity of air when breathing)

Initially, and at times throughout the grief process, survivors experience anxiety and panic. They feel that their lives are spinning out of control. They feel unsafe and fear they will lose others they love. They may find themselves reading obituaries in the paper, wondering if someone else they know has died. An upcoming date of significance in the life of the loved one always produces anxiety. Birthdays, anniversaries of the suicide, and holidays are especially difficult. Most survivors find anticipation of the day is worse than the day itself. Many report that their anxiety is eased and the day is more manageable if they make some special plans for themselves: stay home from work, get a massage, or go to a movie or sports event, for example. "The

366th day was no different to me than the 50th day or the 120th day," recalled a survivor husband. "They were all difficult. But my therapist congratulated me for having survived for a whole year, and I realized that the waves of pain weren't coming as often now and didn't last as long as in the beginning."

> *"I am not afraid of anything anymore! There is nothing that can be worse than losing my son to suicide."*
>
> — Survivor father

Anger/Blame

"I was at the wedding reception of a relative when my mother entered the hall and asked me to come with her into one of the powder rooms," said a survivor named Jackie. "There she told me that my son, Jake, was dead, that he had killed himself. I felt absolutely trapped in that small room, and I wanted to tear the paper right off the walls!"

Anger may be an immediate reaction, but it also plays a necessary role in the processing of grief. Survivors are often afraid to be angry at their loved one, fearing that once they begin they will be unable to stop, that they might hurt themselves or someone else, or that others might view them as weak or crazy. To express anger at the deceased seems a betrayal, yet they probably did so while he or she was alive. It is healthy to express anger in appropriate ways. Anger does not mean the love has ended. It means the survivors are deeply distressed that the loved person is no longer with them.

When Kurt Cobain killed himself, his wife, Courtney, had no problem expressing her anger and sorrow through the media. This allowed Kurt's millions of fans to hear how his suicide affected his family and others, and it may have prevented more suicides by encouraging young people the world over to share their feelings and to mourn openly.

Survivors may feel guilty and blame themselves at first. Or they may blame someone they believe either caused the suicide or could have prevented it. Guilt and blame should diminish, however, with awareness of the process that can lead a person to suicide.

> *"Following the suicide of my beloved partner, Albert, I suffered a unique form of grief. I experienced his death as the ultimate rejection. I was tormented with overwhelming guilt that I wasn't good enough, trusted enough, or loved enough for him to share his agony with me. I thought I could have, should have, been able to save him."*
>
> —JOEL ROTHSCHILD, SURVIVOR AND AUTHOR OF *SIGNALS*

Marie, a survivor mother, said, "I remember how, when Chris was a soldier in the Gulf, I used to drive home every day and pray the military car was not in my driveway to notify me that my son had been killed in action. I never dreamed he would come home safely and then take his own life. I still blame his death, in part, on the post-traumatic stress disorder caused by his experiences in the Gulf War."

Resistance/Avoidance

Survivors may use avoidance behaviors to resist dealing with the pain of grief. This is not unhealthy unless it continues for a long period. Overworking is a common way to avoid grief work. The use of alcohol and drugs is common, but is not helpful in the long term. One woman avoided outside help for an entire year by smoking pot and staying in bed. It took continuous encouragement from a good friend to get her out of the house and into a support group.

At times during the grief process, survivors will be stricken with sudden waves of physical pain, often in the gut or chest, so powerful as to cause them to nearly double over. These will occur without warning and are supremely different from the pain of physical illnesses. These are a reaction to feeling overwhelmed by grief. With time and the proper support, these waves will occur less frequently, be less intense, and last for shorter periods of time.

Immobility/Withdrawal

Often, when avoidance behaviors no longer work to delay mourning, a wave of depression can surface. Anger about the death is kept inside; much energy is used to suppress this anger, and the survivor is left feeling exhausted, defeated, and perhaps searching for purpose and meaning in his own life. "I am alone, ugly, and tired," said a survivor sister named Kathy. "I can't run the store anymore now since Tom died. Now I wish I were dead, too. I hate my life." A survivor daughter echoes her words: "I can't even manage a shower, let alone fix dinner or do laundry for my children. I just want to crawl into bed and stay there." George, a survivor husband, put it this way: "I was living a nightmare and I couldn't wake up."

This depressed state is usually temporary and may occur in the beginning or in the midst of grief. Survivors seek solitude; they often ignore tasks and outings. There is an inability to concentrate, as survivors bear the burden of heightened psychache. Their pain can be so uncomfortable as to cause them to retreat into denial or anger. Care must be taken to ensure they do not get stuck in withdrawal, and that they continue to move forward in the grief journey.

Transition

The numbness, horror, and raw emotions of the first year often seem nearly a blur. By then, most survivors have succumbed to the fact of the loved one's suicide. They are not going to return. The nightmare is real, but life does continue.

> *"The first year is like you're frozen in grief. The second year you begin to thaw out and feel."*
>
> —Sharon, survivor mother

The most acute suffering usually diminishes within the first two years, as survivors heal in small increments. It may take from two to five years to reach the transition stage. Some actually dread reaching the stage where they will feel less pain, as they fear it will mean they are erasing the memories of their loved one.

But with time, perseverance, and support, survivors learn that transition means reinventing their lives without the physical presence of the loved one, while continuing to love and honor that person. They gradually understand that they may release themselves from thinking of the loved one every moment of each day. They have others to love, who also love them, and they have much to live for. They feel again. They accept that they are not—nor will they ever be—the person they were before. They are growing. They are surviving. Their loved one holds a special place in their heart and will never be forgotten.

Helen's sixty-seven-year-old husband shot himself in the family home. She kept his ashes in a glass urn, which she took everywhere with her. She greeted him in the morning and said, "Good night, Ed," when she went to bed. She even took him to their favorite restaurant occasionally and ordered what he liked to eat. Helen talked to him at home, cried about him, yelled at him. One day, as she was sweeping the floor, she thought of how much time she had given to him since his suicide. It was almost more than when he had been alive. She thought of her children and grandchildren, and how little she had seen of them lately. Suddenly she opened the urn, dumped the ashes on the floor, and, "I swept him right out into the clean, fresh, springtime air. It was time. It gave me a sense of comfort and peace. I could live *my* life again!"

Everything Changes

As survivors move back and forth through the grief reactions, many changes occur. Each change brings new grief. One mother thought it would be good to move into the new house the family had bought just before her son's suicide. As the time approached to make the move, she thought of all her son's belongings. She shared her turmoil with her Survivors of Suicide group, crying, "Where will his things go? I'm not ready for my son not to have his own room!"

Relationships change, too. Some friends may be unable to bear hearing the survivor talk and cry about the suicide: it is just too sad. Some people may avoid them, not knowing what to say. Most survivors say that some people who were once friends fade out of the picture, while former or new acquaintances become close friends. But fear of rejection and abandonment can cause survivors to become wary of letting new acquaintances get too close or allowing family members to go too far away. The world doesn't seem safe at this time, and the fear of losing someone else is very near the surface. A sense of more impending doom can cause friction within the family.

"I am broken hearted," wrote a survivor sister in a letter to her loved one. "I can't see you anymore. Everything has changed. Our family has changed since your death. Dad looks horrible—like life has been sucked out of him. Steph is in her own world and doesn't include her husband. She has turned back into her old selfish self. John makes less sense than he ever did. Mom and John argue all the time. Mom has tremendous guilt. I've become a real basket case . . . this is all too much for us."

Indeed, members of a survivor household may experience different levels of grief at a given time. One family member may feel angry while another is withdrawn. Someone else may avoid mourning altogether. The loss has destabilized the family structure, and the difference in their grief reactions makes it even more difficult for them to support each other. Outside resources such as counselors, clergy, and support groups can help to ensure that each person receives the time and support necessary to move through the stage of grief he is experiencing.

Am I Going Crazy?

This is one of the questions survivors ask most. At first, they awaken each morning to a moment of hoping recent events were only a nightmare, but they are freshly grief-stricken when the truth is recalled. They fear they will never feel normal again. They cannot always think clearly, their memories fail them, they "forget" that their loved one is dead and so expect to see him any minute now. The phone rings and they think the loved one is calling. One woman lost a twin son to suicide. Each time she heard or saw the living twin, she was momentarily certain that he was her dead son, that the suicide was only a dream. Survivors worry that they're going crazy, but it is the grief that feels crazy. These are normal people having normal reactions to a situation that is *not* normal. They become overwhelmed, struggling with a mixture of feelings that may be both frightening and immobilizing. Survivors report feeling many different ways, including

abandoned
angry
anxious
cheated
confused
depressed
deserted
despairing
destroyed
disorganized
disoriented
distrustful
embarrassed
exhausted
fearful
forgetful
frustrated
guilty
helpless
hopeless
inadequate
insecure
isolated
lonely
numb
out of control
pained
panicky
powerless
rageful
rejected
relieved
resentful
responsible
shamed
shattered
shocked
suicidal
unloved
unprotected
unworthy
urgent
vulnerable
worried

"At first I couldn't have told you how I felt," said one survivor workshop participant. "I was a hodgepodge of a million feelings. Now that I've seen your list, I think I felt a degree of each of those."

Thoughts of one's own possible suicide

Considering suicide is common for survivors because they are suffering such terrible grief. Generally, survivors do not act on these thoughts, even though they may say they wish they were dead. Such thoughts are usually fleeting, and time should be allowed for them to pass. Talking about these frightening thoughts with others will reduce their power. If you have such thoughts, keep these suggestions in mind.

- Let the thoughts just be there. Choose not to act on them.
- Maybe all you can do now is to live from moment to moment, breathing in and out. That is fine. These thoughts will pass.
- If you can't talk about these feelings, try not to be alone.
- Think about the people you love and care about.
- Think of all the people who love and care for you.
- Call your local crisis center.
- Choose to get through this day alive. Things always change.

Compounded Grief

Suicide grief is especially complex because it often includes factors not found in other types of deaths. These factors range from the death's suddenness to stigma issues to potential post-traumatic stress disorder. Let's examine some of these factors that may compound survivors' grief.

Sudden death

Suicide is always sudden, premature, and nearly always unexpected. Most survivors claim that their loved one was the last person in the world they would have expected to kill himself. They are shocked that they noticed no warning signs. When a death is anticipated, as with a terminal illness, it allows one time to prepare for the loss. Suicide survivors have no such time to prepare. They are dealt a triple blow: the death is sudden, violent, and self-inflicted.

Secret suffering

One of the most difficult truths for the survivor to accept and understand is that their loved one suffered such terrible pain that she killed herself to end it. And she had kept it a secret. Although grasping this truth entails great anguish, eventually, it provides some sense of comfort to realize the loved one is no longer suffering.

Intensity of relationship

As with most grief, the intensity of the relationship determines the intensity of the grief. A husband's suicide would cause a deeper, longer-lasting grief than that of a distant cousin or an acquaintance. The closer and more loving the relationship, the more intense the grief.

No viewing of the body

Many survivors don't ever see the body of the loved one because the casket must be closed or the body cremated. Some bodies are unrecognizable. This prevents some survivors from accepting the reality of the death and may result in prolonged grieving.

Violent death
The death was not only sudden and premature; it was violent either in fact or in the perceptions of the survivors. Even suicides by overdose, perceived by many as a peaceful way to die, contain an element of violence.

Extended mourning
When a family loses someone to accident or illness, other people freely offer support for as long as the family needs it. When a loss is to suicide, survivors report a lack of continued support—which they may need for a much longer period—and the lack of freedom to grieve as long as they need to. Learning about complicated grief helps both the overwhelmed survivors and their support persons understand why the grief process lasts so long.

The stigma of self-inflicted death can make the grief especially intense. This is not to say that survivors suffer more than those individuals who lose people to other types of death, but that they tend to suffer longer and differently.

A sense of rejection
Many survivors believe they have failed somehow to keep their loved one alive. They feel powerless; the question of "why" becomes an obsession. Suicide seems the ultimate

rejection. "My fiancée hung herself the night before our wedding," said a survivor named Marvin. "How could I *not* feel rejected?"

Survivors do not just lose special people who happen to die. No one murdered them, there was no accident. Their loved ones purposefully destroyed themselves.

Stigma

Survivors are further impeded in their healing by labels of blame, shame, and disgrace that our culture attaches to the act of suicide. These are powerful forces. While friends, neighbors, and acquaintances would naturally offer comfort to bereaved families, they cannot always offer the same consolation to survivors of suicide. Though well-meaning, most people are at a loss for words that will not further distress the survivor. In many communities people are critical of the family and even tend to hold the survivors accountable. This lack of understanding and support leaves survivors feeling abandoned and rejected. The isolation that results makes the healing process more painful and problematic. In the words of Janice, a survivor wife, "Everywhere I go, I feel as if people are looking, whispering, and judging."

Post-traumatic stress disorder

Learning of a suicide is horrifying. Survivors who observe the suicide, view the site, discover the body, or smell odors associated with death suffer extreme trauma. They may develop post-traumatic stress disorder (PTSD) symptoms such as anxiety, panic attacks, breathlessness, chest pain, and night terrors. PTSD makes it all but impossible for sufferers to function normally on a daily basis. The scene of their loved one's self-destruction may play over and over in their minds ("daymares").

"Mom's car was in the driveway, but she didn't answer the doorbell," said a survivor named Dan. "When I opened the front door, a horrible smell nearly knocked me down, and then I saw my sixty-two-year-old mother sitting on the sofa, head leaning back. I stood paralyzed, knowing she was dead. I saw the empty pill bottles beside her on the sofa, and an empty wine bottle on the floor. My mom didn't even like wine."

Even survivors who saw nothing of the site may construct a mental scene as powerful as the actual one. One woman discovered her son in the bathroom after he shot himself in the head. Although she was the one to find the body, she was able to deal with the trauma with less difficulty than her husband and her younger son. When she described the death scene to them, they were both relieved to know that the son's head had been turned so that the wound could not be seen. They had imagined a much bloodier scene.

Without appropriate treatment, individuals may be incapable of doing the grief work necessary for healing. Whether or not you have witnessed the scene, there is no need to suffer with the distressing symptoms of PTSD. See a professional to find relief.

The grief that strikes a survivor of suicide can seem insurmountable. However, many survivors, even though their lives are very different now, find themselves healing slowly but surely. They have a new appreciation of life's fragility and preciousness, and they look forward to the future with new hope. They are learning that there is life after suicide, and although they understand it will not be easy, they are determined to live it well.

Five

Healing Well

The goal for survivors is to reinvent their lives without the physical presence of the loved one—while continuing to cherish and remember that person. Mourning, the process of *adapting* to loss, is an action; it is the path through grief. As you travel this path, you will find that successful mourning involves four components: support, willingness, knowledge, and time.

Support

When survivors attempt to put their lives back together, they find it a nearly impossible task. In their lives lurks an enormous empty space in which the spirit of a living, breathing being once resided. Life can never be as it was, but you will find it worth living again. You will put all your love and memories in a special place in your heart. As you learn more about suicide, you will begin to understand the pain your loved one was experiencing. Most survivors endure similar pain during the grief and mourning periods. You may even come to feel some semblance of relief that your loved one no longer suffers the gut-wrenching pain that drove him or her to suicide.

You will change in many ways as your grief journey continues. Eventually, you will create a life that has new purpose and meaning. The sadness will always be just under the surface. But, like millions of other survivors, you *can* heal your life.

How can survivors "heal well"? An important first step is to gather support. Family members and friends may not be a stable source of support at this time, as they may be struggling with their own grief. Outside sources can help, such as family doctors, psychiatrists, psychologists, clergy, counselors, mental health agencies, crisis centers, and grief support groups, especially those that specifically address surviving suicide. Some survivors use combinations of therapies, and many find prescribed medications useful to manage anxiety, sleep and appetite problems, panic, and other symptoms that prevent or delay the process of healing.

"I was barely eighteen when my grandmother killed herself in a motel room," said a survivor named Leslie. "When we found out about it, my grandpa and I drove to the motel. . . . It was the most horrible thing I've ever experienced. My grandfather broke my heart with his wailing. He didn't see the police carry Gram's body out of the motel room without a body bag, but I did, and it was a sight I had nightmares about for months. I did finally go to a therapist, and she helped me to work through the grief. We also had

Gram's body cremated, and my grandpa and I took her ashes to a special place and spread them. I think this helped both of us."

Many survivors are extremely traumatized after a suicide. They may not be aware that they could be suffering from post-traumatic stress disorder. Gary M. Burnett, longtime director of a critical incident response program, describes it:

> Post-traumatic stress, itself, is a normal, predictable psychological reaction to any traumatic event, such as finding a loved one who has completed suicide. This stress is often characterized by intrusive images, sleep disturbance, hyper-vigilance, and avoidance behaviors. An affected individual may further be diagnosed with acute stress disorder or post-traumatic stress disorder (PTSD) depending upon the severity of symptoms and their persistence over time. More severe symptoms such as numbing, depersonalization, flashbacks, and hyper-arousal which significantly impact an individual's daily functioning could be categorized as an acute stress disorder within thirty days from the traumatic event. When symptoms persist beyond thirty days, one may be diagnosed with post-traumatic stress disorder which is the most severe and debilitating type of human stress. Symptoms may include distressing dreams, depression, angry outbursts, hyper-startle reactions,

> and panic attacks. Needless to say, both acute stress disorder and post-traumatic stress disorder require professional assistance.[1]

PTSD may delay the necessary grief work following a suicide. It is important to address the trauma before it becomes a barrier to healing. Patricia Yoder, a clinical psychologist who treats PTSD, discusses its effects:

> Here is an example of how trauma can affect the human body. A woman finds her brother hanging in the garage. The traumatic scene before her is imprinted on her mind. The scene is stuck in her visual field. The horrific image remains fixated day and night. It will play like a movie right in front of her face. If instead of finding the body, the woman remembers the last conversation with her brother, thinking she should have known of his pain, this may replay over and over in her mind. The goal is to move the traumatic scene from the front of the visual field, back into the mind, where the trauma is no longer the focus and the grief work may begin.[2]

Do seek professional help, especially if you feel you are suffering from PTSD. Alternative therapies, too, are available; some sources are listed at the back of this book. And stay open to support from friends and acquaintances. "I was having trouble sleeping at night, and I was uncomfortable sleeping alone in the house during the day," said Tina, a survivor wife. "I told a friend, and she came over every afternoon and stayed while I took a nap."

If you are helping to support a survivor

Keep these ideas in mind when reaching out to a person in grief.

- Listen and allow survivors to talk and cry as much and as often as they need to. Crying and talking are a natural part of mourning, as is describing details of the suicide.
- If you knew the person who died, don't be afraid to talk about that person. This will not cause more hurt than the survivor already feels, and it gives the survivor permission to talk freely about the loved one.
- Small acts of kindness make a significant difference. Run an errand, cook a meal, help around the house, pick the children up from school, or read them stories.
- Continue to offer support for as long as needed.
- Look for a local survivor group. If the survivor is reluctant to attend, offer to go along. Groups offer support, comfort, and validation in a safe environment.
- In some workplaces, co-workers can offer colleagues some of their own vacation time. Since most employers allow for only a few days of bereavement leave, this can be very much appreciated.

One survivor husband received many invitations to dinner from caring friends. Fearing he would burst into tears, he always declined. He was surprised one night to find a meal wrapped in foil inside his mailbox, along with a note that read, "Hi, Al. We understand you need time alone now. We hope you enjoy. From friends who love you, Bob and Ellie." This brought great comfort to Al, and it reminded him that people still cared about him.

Willingness

It's all right to cry as long and as often as you want to for the rest of your life. Give yourself sufficient time to mourn. The suicide of your loved one interrupted your life. Where once there was some kind of order to your days, now chaos reigns. Establishing some routine can provide a sense of normalcy; try resuming an activity you enjoyed before the death.

You need to be willing to seek out and accept support during this period. This may include new experiences with which you are not familiar. Asking for help takes willingness, and it takes courage to be willing. For example, some people believe taking medication is a crutch or a sign of weakness, but in fact it can be a great help, when taken as prescribed. Look beyond any personal bias; be willing to try new ways of healing.

It's okay, even healing, for survivors to enjoy themselves. Allow yourself to have happy moments. Enjoyment does not dishonor or cause you to forget your loved one. A willingness to allow "grief breaks" is healthy.

Knowledge

Education is key to healing well. Learning about the complexities of suicide provides answers to many of the questions haunting survivors. One of the most pressing is *why?* As survivors learn more about the dynamics of the suicidal mind, they grow to understand that the reason for the suicide was the suffocating pain from which their loved one needed desperately to escape. Said Lee, an attempter and survivor, "I believe that when people read about suicide, and talk with other survivors, it teaches them the truth about suicide and eliminates a lot of shame. I had a lot of shame until I started helping other people. It's like 'paying it forward.'"

There are a variety of ways to learn more about suicide. Reading books and articles, talking with other survivors and attending survivor support groups, attending grief or survivor conferences—all are excellent ways to learn about suicide and recovery.

Talk Tip: Some survivors and others avoid the phrase commit suicide, *feeling that it blames the person who died. They prefer phrases such as* complete suicide *or* died by suicide *as a way to reduce stigma. The authors, however, hold the belief that people should talk about suicide in any way they can. The important thing is that they do talk about it.*

Time

Time can never completely heal your wounds, but with support, knowledge, and willingness, time can help you realize that you *are* tolerating your loss. You are healing and moving beyond mere survival. You are finding new ways to think about your loss. You are becoming willing to give up being frozen and afraid. You are searching for a way to give your loss new meaning.

How long does grief last?

This is like asking, "How high is up?" Devastation overwhelms survivors for most of the first year. Their minds cannot comprehend the loss, nor can they imagine what it will mean in the time to come. During this time survivors dwell on the suicide itself, what happened, and why. Thoughts of their loved one never leave their minds as they struggle to get through each day. As the survivor returns to work and daily activities, concentration is difficult if not impossible at times. The mind is furiously trying to cope with the feelings generated by the suicide, and living is one moment at a time.

> *Survivors often describe the second year as "the year of thawing out."*

After the first year, the focus of grief changes from intellectualizing the loss. Now, the myriad feelings that were relegated to the unconscious mind begin to emerge. Survivors are surprised at the fierceness of these feelings. They hoped they were getting better. They describe this phase of healing as *the year of thawing out.* Friends and family who have expected them to be "themselves" again are disappointed and frustrated by this new wave of grief. If not dealt with appropriately, emotional stress is held in the body and eventually expressed as some form of physical pain. Most survivors have visited their health care practitioners by now with some physical complaint.

With support, knowledge, willingness, and time, a sense of stability returns. It may take from two to five years to recover from this complicated grief process. Now survivors don't feel the intense pain every minute. They can begin to enjoy periods of time without guilt. They will never forget their loved ones, but they don't need to think about them constantly, and, gradually, they have more good days than bad.

Remember, there is no exact time frame for the grief journey. Give yourself permission to grieve for as long or as short a time as you need.

Healing Well

Take care of your body, mind, and soul. Use these ideas to help yourself "heal well."

Ask for what you want

Overwhelmed by grief, survivors may wish for privacy, company, assistance with a task, a hug, or something else for which they don't ask. Start asking. You will most likely get what you want, and it may help to move your grief journey forward. If you don't ask for or accept help, others may interpret this as a wish to be left alone.

Exercise

Physical activity releases "feel-better" chemicals into your body. You don't have go to the gym four times a week to reap the benefits of exercise. Even walking produces a feeling of well-being and increases energy. Make a decision to walk just five minutes today. Walking daily for as long as you feel comfortable can have a healing influence on grief.

Laugh

Though survivors initially say they feel guilty laughing while their loved ones lie dead, they also say that when they begin to laugh again, they feel better and lighter. Research shows that laughter is healing. For some, laughter leads to tears, which is a healthy way to release feelings. It's good to watch humorous movies or television comedy shows. Spend time with people who like to have fun. Schedule a little time at first, then more as you realize that it is okay to enjoy yourself again.

Honor your memories

Survivors do better when they embrace the memories of the deceased. You can keep photographs of your loved one out where you and everyone can see and enjoy them. Celebrate his birthday in some special way. Make a scrapbook. You don't have to forget your loved one or live your life without thinking about and loving him. Some survivors set a place for their loved one at the table on holidays. Watch videos of him. Talk about him. Talk *to* him. The fact that he isn't physically here anymore does not decrease your love. He is still in your heart. You have spent so much time remembering how he died. It's okay to remember how he lived.

Self-care

Taking good care of yourself is always important, but it is probably more vital now than at any other time in your life. Stress inhibits the immune system, and you may find yourself feeling ill or exhausted. With all the mental and emotional chaos going on right now, you need to stay healthy. There are many things that will help you feel more energetic and well. Try a few of these suggestions:

- Rest, even if you don't sleep. If sleep is a problem, talk with your health care practitioner.
- Take a multivitamin each day.
- Keep a glass of water near you and drink several glasses a day.
- Eat nourishing foods that you love.
- Have a friend, relative, or cleaning service help around the house every once in a while.
- Attend a grief support meeting.
- Get a foot or body massage.
- Light a candle and take a long, hot bath.
- Go to lunch with a friend.

- Go for a walk.
- Read a good book.
- Listen to music you love.
- Put your feet up, relax, and talk to a friend on the phone.
- Watch a funny video or movie.
- Go to your loved one's grave site and talk to her.

You may not feel like it, but you are healing a tiny bit each day. Feeling the pain is part of healing the pain. Remember, you have permission to cry as often and as long as you like for the rest of your life.

Get active

As soon as you're ready, try to return to activities you once enjoyed, or take part in a new group activity. Take up tennis, swimming, scrapbooking, painting, crafting, anything that will help you feel good about yourself and enhance your social life. Many survivors work with suicide prevention groups as a way to feel better and to help others. You get to choose what your "new normal" will be.

Linda, a survivor mother, described her own healing journey. "Several months after my son's death, my therapist instructed me to develop a list of things I'd always wanted to do. That was such a good assignment. We concluded I could live without raising a cougar or learning to fly, and so I focused on getting my master's degree. Going back to school opened me up to new friends and new ideas, and eventually, when I began writing my thesis, I selected youth suicide for the topic. That decision resulted in my learning so much that helped me understand the enigma and the complexity and the amazing history of suicide and its study. In a way, I had been 'trying on a lot of hats' for a year or so, and I finally began to find some that fit, which was very healing."

Be willing to forgive

Every survivor feels varying degrees of hurt, anger, blame, and rejection. These feelings may be directed at oneself or at others. Survivors need not ever forgive anyone or anything . . . unless they seek peace. Negative, hateful feelings can eat away at one's well-being. Without forgiveness, they continue their destructive path until the survivor and those around him are miserable and lonely.

It is a huge challenge for survivors to forgive themselves or others on whom they have heaped blame and resentment. But the opportunity is there. A desire to forgive someone will not make it happen; but *willingness* to forgive is the first step in the process. Forgiveness happens within the heart. It is an act of grace and leads to that for which all survivors yearn: peace and acceptance.

The benefits of forgiveness

- releases the negative energy of blame, fear, anger, and hate
- allows feelings of love to return
- brings peace to the mind and heart
- releases fear
- makes it possible to accept the unacceptable

- returns peace and freedom to you and those closest to you
- It is never too early or too late to forgive.

Practice forgiveness

- Write a letter expressing all your feelings of anger, fear, blame, and hurt. Read it to a trusted friend or professional, then destroy it.
- Decide to stop punishing yourself or others. Recognize that those who need your forgiveness are providing the opportunity for you to learn to forgive. When you forgive others, you are also forgiving yourself, creating peace and freedom.
- Keep in mind that forgiving does not mean that you condone the actions of others.
- Read and talk with others about forgiveness.

Growing into forgiveness

Dennis Liegghio's song lyrics, "No Resolve," can be found in the front of this book. His story illustrates the power of forgiveness for survivors who wish to move on with their lives.

> I think we've all said awful things to our parents while we were kids. Things like "I hate you and I never want to talk to you again!" I was young and angry when I said that to my dad. I didn't really mean it. I didn't even fully understand what I was saying. I was fourteen, and those were the last words I ever said to my father. Three months later, he

downed a bunch of pills, slit his wrists, and drove himself into a tree.

I don't remember much of it, really; it's mostly a blur . . . it was a lifetime ago. By the time this book is printed, it will have been sixteen years. I do know that I went though a whole lot of alcohol and drugs and women. I know that I released most of my anger and sadness through self-destructive activities that broke my mother's heart and put my life in serious jeopardy. After I was through hating God so much, I stopped believing in Him. I truly thought I would be dead before I was twenty-five, and I didn't care.

I hadn't touched my guitar or written a song for a few years, until one night in 2002, when I picked up the guitar and began playing. I found myself singing about the suicide of my dad, and how it had hurt me. The feelings poured out of me in the form of lyrics, and in a short time I had written a song from my heart. I titled the song "No Resolve," and singing it changed something in me. I recorded it on an old four-track recorder in my basement, along with a few other songs I wrote soon after. When my friends heard the record, they liked it. I had never had the courage to let others hear my music before, and they were responding positively. It felt magical to me. The more I opened myself up to others, the more emotions I was able to put to music.

I started a band. We dedicated our first album to my father and put his picture in the liner notes. We went on the road; we played shows and it felt good. It made me feel good that so many people loved the song "No Resolve," and that they told me how it impacted them. Those people helped me to finally realize that I was not alone. Others felt as I did.

Over the next few years, I gradually became happier. I worked through some anger, started cleaning up my act, and spent a lot of time trying to figure out my insides. I started caring about myself. I began to see things more clearly . . . what I want to do with my life, and what I don't. I talk openly with my brother and my mother for the first time in years. Things seem to be falling into place for me.

I don't regret anything about my past. If I could go back and change anything, I wouldn't. I wouldn't be who or where I am today without having experienced everything that happened . . . even the pain. I miss my father. It still hurts, especially when something big is happening in my life. But I don't hate him anymore, and I've forgiven him for what he did. I know that he's out there somewhere, looking over me, and he has probably saved my life a number of times over the past several years. I know that somehow, he can hear my song, every time I play it. I'm nearly thirty years old now. Five years older than I thought I'd ever be. Writing that song has literally saved my life. Maybe it can save someone else's too.[3]

Six

Staying Alive

It is correct to say that anyone thinking of taking his own life is certainly experiencing some sort of mental distress. But it would not be correct to say that one must have a mental illness in order to think about, or die by, suicide.

Depressed individuals should absolutely be identified and treated appropriately for their illness, and this undoubtedly helps prevent some suicides. But as we have seen, suicide is a matter of unbearable psychache *plus* the simultaneous idea of death as the only solution. Many people undergo suggested treatment options for clinical depression and other mental distress and still take their own lives. Depression and suicide are different "animals." And since most depressed individuals can live long, unhappy lives, we need to know more than the symptoms of depression if we want to prevent suicide. We must learn the signs of impending suicide.

We must also sort the myths from the realities of the issue. The information in this chapter is adapted in part from *The Psychology of Suicide* by Edwin Shneidman, Norman Farberow, and Robert Litman.[1]

Myths about Suicide

Myths and misconceptions continue to cloud the issue of suicide today, despite tremendous efforts in recent years to educate the public about the facts as we know them. Examining these myths causes some survivors to feel guilt, but they could not have acted on information they did not have at the time. By exploring these myths, survivors learn more facts about suicide and reducing its stigma. We will never prevent all suicides. But just as knowing how and when to perform cardiopulmonary resuscitation—CPR—allows a person to intervene in a potentially lethal situation, so dispelling the myths about suicide raises our awareness of potentially suicidal symptoms and behaviors, and perhaps our ability to intercede to save lives.

Myth 1: People who talk about suicide don't do it.

All talk or threats of suicide should be taken seriously. Some people believe that the threat is a means of getting attention. So be it. Giving someone appropriate attention when they talk of death is a most effective way to prevent suicide. Even those who have tried for months or years to support a loved one who continues to talk about or attempt suicide are shocked when it finally occurs. Most suicidal individuals rarely warn their friends and families directly; instead, they may offer vague verbal clues, usually to people who are not in a position to help them. If suicides are to be prevented, any suggestion, sign, or threat of suicide must be taken seriously. Even though individuals may have made threats or left clues before, this may be the time they die. Action must always be taken when a threat is perceived, even if there is doubt that the person is serious. Still, there is no guarantee that the suicidal person will not complete his plan even when clues are noticed and addressed appropriately.

Young people often reveal their suicidal thoughts to a friend, but they may not be taken seriously. One survivor mother said, "After his death, I learned that Ronald had confessed to four of his good friends and one school counselor that he didn't want to live anymore. He was obviously begging for help. No one believed him . . . and not one of them said anything to me!"

Myth 2: Suicidal people want to die.

Suicidal individuals are suffering severe mental and psychological pain. They are not so much seeking death as craving the peace of unconsciousness, escaping their constant feelings of utter distress. Many spend much of their lives searching for ways to relieve their pain so they won't have to die. When the suffering becomes unbearable, and if nothing they have tried reduces it, then there may appear to be *only* one way to relieve it. Suicidal individuals do not desire death over life. They need to be free of pain.

Myth 3: Once suicidal, always suicidal.

Nearly everyone has had a suicidal thought at some point in their lives and did not act on it. Indeed, most suicidal episodes are short-lived. An individual may suffer powerful thoughts of suicide once in his life, pass through that period, and never have another suicidal thought. Some who have considered killing themselves have been saved by a kind or coincidental act that reduced their psychache and self-destructive thoughts. Acts of fate, circumstance, fortuity, and pure chance have probably saved or prolonged thousands of lives. An unexpected visit, a hug, a phone call, or some kindness may offer a small reprieve of time during which other options can be considered.

Myth 4: Using the word suicide *may cause someone to do it.*
Talking about suicide does not make it a prospect in the minds of others. Unless a person is already considering the act, the word *suicide* will only bring to mind their personal feelings and opinions about the topic. It is actually advisable to talk about suicide to suicidal individuals, as this gives them unspoken permission to express their feelings and the opportunity to accept help. If and when the day ever comes when we can all openly talk about suicide without disgust or trepidation, perhaps we can look forward to fewer suicides.

Myth 5: When a distressed person's behavior suddenly improves dramatically, the danger of suicide is over.
To the contrary. If a person who has been chronically sad, angry, withdrawn, or troubled suddenly appears happy, laughing, lighthearted, and "back to normal," family and friends tend to see it as an improvement, a welcome sign of progress. But in reality, the abruptness of the mood shift can be a danger signal. The common manner in which individuals heal from long periods of mental suffering is to gradually

improve. An "overnight" lifting of the spirit often means that the person has planned his suicide down to the last detail and is feeling relieved that his pain will soon end. He might seem like his old self again, perhaps making plans for the future, and this will fool everyone.

The mind of the suicidal person is deep within the tunnel. His thoughts are still constricted. Though the pain is still there, he can tolerate it temporarily as he carries out his plan to die.

Myth 6: People who kill themselves are losers.

Nothing is further from the truth. They may be leaders, excellent students, talented, intelligent, "normal," beautiful, and get along well with others. Many survivors feel that the loved one's problems were "just the normal ones." This is why it is common to hear comments such as these:

"He was the last person in the world I thought would kill himself."

"I can't believe he was feeling so awful."

"She had everything to live for."

"She was planning her wedding!"

"He just started a new job."

"How could she leave her two small children?"

The frightening fact is that suicide knows absolutely no boundaries. It occurs in people of all ages, races, genders, intelligence levels, talents, and lifestyles. One has only to talk with survivors to begin to understand that no one is the "type" to die by suicide.

Warning Signs

Even so, we can name some risk factors and warning signs. Of course, not all will apply to every suicidal person, and in some cases the signs are subtle. But awareness of them could help loved ones perceive danger and possibly intervene.

Risk Factors and Warning Signs of Suicide

Previous attempts
Family history of suicide
Conflicts
Shift in behavior and/or substance use
Withdrawal
Recent meaningful loss
Hopelessness and helplessness
Anxiety
Preoccupation with death
Preparing for death
Sudden lifting of mood

A previous suicide attempt is thought to be one of the most significant risk factors for suicide. A prior attempt may be seen as a trial run, a rehearsal. Many people who have previously attempted suicide eventually complete the act. Some families do not learn that their loved one had previously attempted suicide until after the death.

A family history of suicide is considered a risk factor, as it may be experienced by a suicidal person as permission to follow a pattern. It also models a tragic solution to turmoil and psychological pain. The previous death of a family member by suicide is another factor to consider if you are concerned about the recent behaviors of a loved one.

Conflicts within the home, family, in close relationships, or with the law cause added turmoil in the lives of suicidal individuals, increasing the burden of psychache they must bear. We all have some conflict in our lives, but for suicidal persons, increased conflict can heighten psychological pain beyond their tolerance.

A shift in behavior and/or substance use is seen in some suicidal persons. Increased recklessness or impulsivity is a concern especially if it includes more use of alcohol or drugs, a refusal to take prescribed medications, and/or refusal to accept help or talk about what they are feeling.

Withdrawal from family, friends, and usual activities is a sign that something has changed within the mind of a loved one. This may present as more time spent alone, watching TV, reading, on the computer, or in the workshop. A vague reason may be given for this change in behavior.

A recent meaningful loss has occurred prior to many suicides. The loss may be that of a close relationship, a job, a pet, health, some type of personal freedom, self-esteem, or anything the suicidal person perceives she cannot live without. It is not this particular loss that causes the suicide. It is this loss, the last in a series of events or perceptions, which has driven the psychache within the mind of this person to an unendurable level.

All changes in a person's behavior mean something!

While the above signs may seem subtle, it is always a good idea to address them with the person. It is most important to remember that all change means something. Determine the meaning of any changes of which you become aware.

Hopelessness and helplessness. These are perhaps the most dangerous feelings that haunt the suicidal mind. When there is no hope that things will get better, no hope that anything can take away the crushing pain, when one feels helpless to change his circumstances, he ultimately believes there is no use in continuing to try. He banishes himself to his own mind, where the drama is playing out in loneliness, isolation, and pain beyond imagining.

There is nothing as dangerous to the suicidal mind as the perception of hopelessness. When a person is in a state of hopelessness, the word *only* is commonly used in ways such as these:

"It's the *only* choice I have."

"I can *only* take so much."

"If I could *only* have it (her/him/my job) back."

"It's the *only* way out."

Some level of anxiety is often seen with suicidal thinking. Anxiety is an extremely difficult feeling to tolerate for any length of time. This type of anxiety is not mere nervousness or restlessness, although they may be the first physical signs one sees. Anxiety may occur at any time during the progression of suicidal thoughts, and since there is good medical treatment for anxiety, there is no reason for anyone to suffer from it. It is possible that prompt treatment for anxiety can prevent some suicides.

Preoccupation with death is perhaps the most obvious warning sign, although it does not precede every suicide. This can present in several ways, and it may be a subconscious plea for help. For example, the person may talk about death by using statements that are similar to the following:

"Will I see Dad when I get to heaven?"

"I hope I don't wake up in the morning."

"I hate my life."

"Nobody would care if I wasn't here anymore."

"I'm just an old man, no use to anyone."

Some of these statements are vague and may have nothing to do with suicide, so each needs to be put into perspective. What is going on in that person's life right now? What other signs do you see? Has there been a recent loss? Is the person starting to use alcohol or drugs, or increasing such use? Have you asked about thoughts of suicide? No statements are irrelevant. A follow-up discussion is absolutely necessary. Assume nothing.

Often a suicidal individual will listen to music about death; talk, write poetry, or journal about death; or draw pictures of death scenes. The person may question the meaning or purpose of life, or wonder why he or she is here.

Preparing for death in practical terms, the person may

give away personal items, write a will, or set personal affairs in order.

A sudden lifting of mood, as noted earlier, can sometimes occur when a person has internally made the suicide decision. Ironically, friends and family may perceive this as a good sign, but it could imply that the next step will be fatal.

Suicidal people may display all, a few, or none of the behaviors discussed above, making it important to pay close attention to significant changes in their behaviors. At this time we cannot predict who will kill themselves. There is no test or technique that can determine who is likely to die by suicide.

Mental or psychological distress, anxiety, perturbation, and anger must always be addressed. These signs are signals that the person is dealing with psychache that may be advancing to a dangerous level. If there is concern that someone may be thinking of suicide, there is a way to find out.

If you or someone you know feels suicidal, please call the National Suicide Prevention Lifeline:

1-800-273-TALK (1-800-273-8255)

Ask the question

If you are uncertain whether a person is having suicidal thoughts, the simplest and most effective way to find out is to ask in a direct, kind manner. It may be difficult, but this question, more than anything else that might be said, has the potential to save a life. Asking this question will *not* put the idea in someone's mind. To the contrary, it is most often a relief for the suicidal individual to know he can finally talk about his secret to someone who will listen. He has now been given direct permission to speak the unspeakable.

There are many ways in which to ask this crucial question. A few suggestions follow:

"I am wondering if you ever think of ending your life."

"Sometimes people who are going through what you are now think about suicide. Are you thinking of suicide?"

"Have you been having suicidal thoughts?"

"Are you thinking of killing yourself?"

How *not* to ask the question:

"You're not thinking of suicide, are you?"

"You aren't thinking of doing something stupid, are you?"

"You aren't thinking of hurting yourself, are you?"

Asking in a negative way may tell the person that you do not want to hear the truth or may not be capable of listening to his truthful answer. Using the word *hurt* leaves an "out" for the person to deny suicidal thoughts, as he is not thinking of just "hurting" himself, but of killing himself. Best not to take that chance.

What if the answer is "yes"?

If you learn that a person *is* considering suicide, you must be prepared to follow up with a few more necessary actions. These suggestions may help you talk with a person you have just learned is suicidal:

- Do not panic. You cannot help anyone if you are not in your right mind.
- Do not judge. Regardless of your own feelings for this person or about suicide in general, this is an opportunity to help a person who may be desperate.
- Listen calmly. The goal is for the person to talk about his plight.
- Do not argue. Let him say whatever he needs to say.
- Do not try to "fix" him. Just listen.
- Do not be sworn to secrecy about anything.
- Do not discount his feelings. Feelings are neither right or wrong.
- Tell him you think he must be hurting to be considering suicide.
- Be caring and compassionate.
- Listen, listen, listen. Silence is okay. Phrases such as "Go on . . ." or "Then what happened?" can encourage the person to share his feelings.
- Ask how he intends to kill himself, when, and if he has obtained the means (this might be a gun, pills, rope, car, and so on). If he has, suggest giving that item to a trusted person to keep for now.

- Do not try to solve his problems, but explore options other than suicide.
- Ask if there is a trusted person who can help. If not, suggest 911, a local crisis line, or a hospital emergency room.
- If he has planned the time he will act, and/or has the means, do not leave a suicidal person alone.
- If you are unable for any reason to ask the question or to talk with the suicidal person, tell an adult, a family member, or a professional of your concerns immediately.

The above suggestions are not the only ways to deal with a suicidal person; however, they can be tools for intervening in a potentially life-threatening situation. If you ask the suicide question and the person says no, you have lost nothing. If the answer is yes, you have an opportunity to help. Remember, the vast majority of people do answer truthfully when asked if they are suicidal.

What to do if you suspect someone is suicidal

- Take all direct or indirect comments or clues about suicide seriously.
- Don't be afraid to ask if the person is having suicidal thoughts.
- Stay calm and nonjudgmental.
- Don't leave the suicidal person alone.
- Seek support and guidance from someone the person trusts.

- Suggest calling a mental health professional, a crisis line, clergy person, family member, friend, 911, or an emergency room.

If you *are thinking about suicide*
"I wouldn't be here today if my husband had not unexpectedly walked into the room," said Pat, a near fatality. "I felt hopeless and believed he and the children would be better off without me. It has taken a while, but I'm finally thankful to be alive."

If you are considering suicide, please consider these points and take them to heart.

- Communicate with the people who care about you. They cannot read your mind; they cannot know how badly you are hurting unless you tell them. Say to them straight out, "I am thinking of killing myself, and I don't know what to do. Please help me figure this out." Make them believe how much you need help right now. Don't stop seeking help until someone believes you and comes to your aid.
- Tell others what you need in order to feel better. Survivors always say that they would have done anything to keep their loved ones alive. You can say, "I need to tell someone what I'm thinking of doing." Tell them how you are feeling and what is making you hurt so much.
- Know that there are other ways to resolve your pain. Believe that this is so, and ask someone to help you

figure it out. There is no shame in hurting, and asking for help takes courage. One way to ask is to say, "I don't know exactly how to say this, but I'm hurting very much inside. If I don't feel better soon, I may kill myself."

- Do not believe anyone will be better off without you alive. They won't. They will be devastated and changed forever. Imagine if someone *you* love died by suicide today. If you feel this way, you can tell someone, "I'm not sure why I think everyone would be better off if I was dead, but that's the way I feel now. I don't want to feel this way, so I need some kind of help."
- Know that many people care about you and cannot imagine that you are thinking of suicide. Put the idea of suicide away for now, and talk with people you care about. You might say something like, "I feel like nobody really cares about me." Try to remember that no matter how you feel right now, people do care about you.
- You can have a fulfilling life, no matter what you have done or what has been done to you in the past. Stay alive for now, and take responsibility for changing what you don't like about your life.
- Things will feel different soon. Everyone hurts sometimes. You are hurting now, and that is understandable. Your thinking has become narrowed so that you cannot think about the future. But with work, help, and time, things will feel different. This is a promise.

A Jar of Stones

If you filled a quart jar with small stones, then held it straight out in front of you, you would find that with each passing moment the jar would seem heavier. The weight of the stones did not change, but your arm would hurt more and more until the pain spread to your shoulder, neck, and back and became unbearable. Suppose you wish the people around you to think you are strong enough to hold the jar forever, so when someone talks to you or offers help, you smile and refuse. You pretend everything is fine, even though by now you are in excruciating pain.

Why not allow your friends and family to support your arm or even remove some of the stones from the jar? Would you be ashamed that you could not bear the pain alone? Ashamed that you need help? Ashamed to ask for help?

This is how many suicidal people feel as they scream inwardly for help, but they will neither ask for it nor admit they are hurting. There are many people who would rush to take the jar from you if only they knew that you and your jar of stones were about to crash to the earth.

When a suicide occurs, we survivors are astounded to learn that our loved ones had struggled with a jar of stones that caused them such enormous pain. Each of us is left with a shattered jar that cannot be put back together. We scurry to gather the scattered stones, frantically examining each in hopes of magically seeing what caused our loved one to suffer silently and alone. But the stones hold no answers, and the jar is forever broken. We survivors must work, even kicking and screaming, to heal the scars on our hearts, so that we may hold the beautiful memories of our loved ones there. We finally get back in touch with our own spirits, which, after all, is what we have always been . . . pure spirits dressed in human bodies. The spirits of our loved ones never leave us. They are here to comfort us anytime we stop to listen.

Seven

Connections

What the caterpillar calls the end of the world,
the Master calls a butterfly.

—Richard Bach

This chapter contains stories from survivors who have, in various ways, experienced a connection with their loved one following a suicide. Some communications are subtle but meaningful. Many connection events are so powerful that they leave no doubt in the minds of survivors that their loved one is in a safe and peaceful place. Most of these stories were told in survivor healing groups, as they are one of the few places survivors know they will not be laughed at or scorned. First one person timidly reveals an account of an emotional connection with her loved one, then another survivor shares an experience. Soon they are joined by others who talk of their own inspiring accounts. These stories are important to survivors since they offer a measure of peace and hope to those who are despairing in a suicide's aftermath.

Gabe
1975–1997

In November 2003, I came home from a Survivors of Suicide group feeling so sad that I went to bed early and cried. I lay in the dark, thinking how much I missed my son Gabe. I longed for him to let me know he was okay.

Gabe was twenty-two when he died seven years ago. I have dreamed of him many times since his suicide, but sometime early that morning I had a different kind of dream.

I was in the middle of an outdoor party, still married to Gabe's father, Johnny, and we were down by the water with friends. We heard screams coming from the house, and we ran inside to find our younger son, Brennan, pointing into the kitchen. In the kitchen we saw Gabe! He was beautiful. I began screaming, and I passed out. The next thing I knew, I was in Gabe's arms and I was crying and hysterical. I kept saying, "I know I'm dreaming . . . and you're not really here."

Gabe asked me to calm down. He told me that he was really here, that this wasn't a dream. That he had only a few minutes and he needed me to calm down so that he could tell me something. Oh, it was so wonderful to hold him. I kept running my fingers through his hair and begging him not to leave. Still holding me, Gabe said, "When you think of me, I want you to think of me in Alaska." I became upset and confused and thought he was telling me that he wasn't really dead . . . just hiding out in Alaska. Gabe again asked me to calm down and listen. He said that he wasn't really in Alaska, but that was where he wanted me to think of him being. He said, "Alaska is the only place that is as pure, clean, peaceful, and beautiful as where I really am."

I was still confused. We continued to hold each other and he said, "Don't blame Dad for what happened to me." I immediately said that I didn't blame his dad, but Gabe looked right into my eyes and said, "Yes, Mom, you do, and it wasn't his fault."

There was no time to argue because he said, "I have one more thing and I'm running out of time."

He continued, "Let this go! Let go of your obsession with the way I died!"

I said I didn't understand, and he said, "Yes you do, and you will know."

At this point, my husband, Alan, woke me up, concerned that I was crying in my sleep. I asked him to turn on the light because I was sure I must still have some of Gabe's hair in my hand. I didn't, but the "dream" had been so real that I couldn't stop crying for a while.

The next weekend, I called Gabe's dad to tell him about the "visit" from Gabe. When I mentioned the Alaska part, Johnny began crying. He said that the month before Gabe died, he talked about leaving town and going to Alaska . . . that he just wanted to get the hell out of here and go up there and start over.

A week later, I spoke about suicide prevention at a meeting for counselors, which usually made me feel tired, but good. I left the meeting feeling sick inside. Then I remembered Gabe telling me, "Let it go. You'll know what I mean." He was telling me that it was time to start remembering the way he lived, instead of the way he died. His visit changed my pain so much! I still hurt, and I always will. But I believe he was here, that he came to finish his work and to help me.

I am taking Gabe's advice and letting go of working so hard. I will spend more time with my family. Last weekend Alan and I went to Hurricane Ridge in the mountains. It was a gorgeous day—sunshine, blue sky, and beautiful white snow. I felt so close to Gabe there!

I absolutely believe that Gabe came to me. I think he has finished his work here. And I believe that when my time comes, we will be together again.

Tom
1977–2002

My brother Tom used to have a thing with spare change. It was everywhere, in his truck, in his pockets, in his apartment, in boxes of his stuff. He never gathered it up and used it to buy anything; he just let it accumulate everywhere. After he died and my family and I were cleaning out his truck, we joked that Tom would not have had any money problems if he had just gathered up his spare change.

Almost immediately following Tom's suicide, I began to find spare change everywhere—*in public restrooms, on sidewalks, in every imaginable place at work. I talked to Tom time and again. "Listen, jackass, stop sending me the small stuff, it'll never get me out of debt. Send me paper money or help me win the lottery."*

One afternoon, I visited Tom's grave. There was a penny on his headstone. I picked up the penny and yelled at Tom, "Damn it, Tom, what am I supposed to do with this change?" Then a feeling of "knowing" passed over me, I repeated softly, "What am I supposed to do with this? Change?" *Suddenly, I got it. I realized Tom was making me aware that I needed to make some changes in my life. I needed to change my job, my living arrangements, my habits, my poor decisions, my perceived helplessness, my just-coasting-through life. What a wonderful message for me. I have cherished my message from Tom. It has changed my life and the way I look at death. I truly believe Tom is in a safe and loving place now and that I will see him again some day.*

Andy
1977–2001

Kiara, my three-year-old granddaughter, was in a room adjoining my son Andy's the night he shot and killed himself. She had to be carried out of the room right past Andy's body. Kiara thought Andy was sick because she saw the blood and thought it was "throw up." On the day of the funeral, Andy's fiancée and I were talking about Andy and crying. Having had no experience with church or religion, Kiara totally surprised us by saying, "You guys don't cry. Andy is safe with Jesus now."

A few days after the funeral, I was sitting in Andy's bedroom, when Kiara called to me. She came to the bedroom door and said, "Grandma, can you feel Andy in this room?" Then she said, excitedly, "I need a pencil and paper," which I gave her. She began scribbling all over the paper until she had filled the page. When she was finished, she handed the paper to me and said, "Here you go, Grandma, this is from Andy, read it to me." I looked at her somber little three-year-old face, and at her scribbling, and I told her I thought it said that Andy loved us very much, and missed us. But Kiara frowned and told me, "No, I don't think so, Grandma. I think it says 'I'm sorry I had a gun in the house.'"

I am completely convinced that Andy used Kiara, whom he dearly loved, to tell me he was sorry. And he has used other ways to contact me since.

Kurt
1973–2000

I have always given each of my four children a special ornament for Christmas that reflected what was going on in their lives at the time. The year my son, Kurt, was married, I gave them a clear glass heart inscribed with the words, "Our First Christmas Together, 1999." That year all my children were together, and we had a warm, wonderful Christmas Day at my home. Less than five months later, Kurt killed himself, his wife moved away, and all our lives changed.

For the next two years I was in too much pain to think about Christmas. During this time, I learned that other survivors had created new traditions after suffering the loss of a loved one, and I finally decided that I could do the same. I shared my plans with my daughters in November, and we met for lunch and then strolled in a nearby mall. There were Christmas trees everywhere, all decorated in different themes. We stopped beside one to reminisce about the ornaments I had given the girls in the past. I happened to glance down and saw that one of my daughters was about to step on something on the floor. I bent down to pick it up and found myself holding a clear glass heart that read, "Our First Christmas Together, 1999"! My heart stopped. The three of us were startled beyond words. We walked all over the mall looking for a tree with a heart theme or the brand of ornaments I had always given them.

That year we celebrated on Christmas Eve, and on Christmas we helped serve the less fortunate. Finding that ornament seemed like Kurt was sending his approval of our decision to enjoy the holidays and that he would be with us still, if only in spirit. I keep the heart, Kurt's heart, where I can see it every day to remind myself to cherish his message and to remember that he is always around.

Kevin
1977–2000

Kevin was my youngest son. He died by suicide at the age of twenty-two. He was a free spirit, loving and sensitive. While Kevin was growing up, we had a black Lab named Mindy. Kevin and Mindy had a strong bond, and would lie on the floor nose-to-nose, Kevin petting and stroking the dog. Mindy slept on Kevin's bed every night. Kevin always tried to get me to pet Mindy, but I wasn't a dog person. I was glad Kevin had a dog he loved, but I couldn't pet her or have her on my bed. Sadly, in 1999, Mindy died.

The following year, Kevin killed himself. It was the worst thing that has ever happened to us. Six months after Kevin's death, my husband, Ralph, talked about getting a black Lab puppy, but I didn't think it was a good idea. That very evening Ralph had a dream. In the dream, Kevin appeared and handed Ralph a black Lab puppy, saying, "Dad, do you remember when Mindy used to protect our house?" Next to Kevin stood the pastor of the parish where Ralph and I had grown up, in Detroit. He said, "You know, Ralph, sometimes you have to listen to your children."

I still believe it was a signal from Kevin that he knew we would understand. We got a new black Lab puppy, Savana Rose, and guess where she sleeps? Yes, right on the bed with us. Imagine my amazement that I love and pet her. When my cousin came to visit with her Newfoundland, who was begging me to pet her, I laughed and said to Kevin, "Don't you think you are pushing me a bit too far?" Who would ever have believed I would have a dog I loved? Thank you, Kevin.

Scott
1959–2003

I walked in the house one night to find my fiancé lying on the floor in a pool of blood, a shotgun lying near his body. After the shock and horror subsided, it became my quest to find out if Scott was in heaven. I couldn't stand the thought of him just being in the ground or someplace where he hadn't found the peace I know he needed.

I never enjoyed hiking, but Scott did, and I would go just to be with him. One afternoon while we were standing in one of his favorite places in the nearby state park, he told me that if he ever died, I would find his spirit soaring like an eagle in this place. Six months after he passed, I was feeling inconsolable so I went to the park to try to find his spirit as an eagle. As soon as I arrived there, I saw an eagle, but I didn't feel anything special because there were always eagles there.

Next I went to talk with our pastor, who assured me Scott was in heaven, but I left there unconvinced. I needed to know for sure. I prayed and asked Scott to help me with this.

When Scott and I were together, we had a little game we played. If either of us found a penny, we would pick it up and keep it in our wallet for good luck. When we found another penny, we replaced the one in our wallet, and threw the previous penny over a shoulder for someone else to find. Scott would do this and would come home and tell me that he had found a new good luck penny. It was kind of a fun thing for us.

The night I came home from talking with our pastor, I was cleaning some candle wax off the glass kitchen table, and I no-

ticed something on the floor next to one of the legs. I will never forget the flood of joy as I picked up a penny, but it was no ordinary penny. Someone had cut the center of the penny into the shape of an angel in a flowing gown. The date was still readable, and it was 1998, the very same year Scott and I started a committed relationship. The previous day I had swept my hardwood floors and nobody had been in my house since. I can't tell you how deeply I felt that I had found what I had been seeking. For me, this penny, which I always wear on a chain around my neck, confirms that my Scott is somewhere, peaceful and safe.

Tyler
1967–2004

My wife, Tyler, completed suicide on Saturday evening, January 17, 2004, by hanging herself from our open staircase while I was in the shower. Tyler was thirty-seven years old, a former model, and a law school graduate. Tyler had developed a significant bond with my search and rescue dog, Riggs. She loved and cared for Riggs and allowed him to support her emotional needs when I was away. Tyler's world began to significantly unravel after Riggs's death in December 2002.

In June 2004, five months after Tyler's suicide, I traveled to Iceland. The weather was terrible for several days, and I was miserable, thinking about Tyler and Riggs and that my entire family was gone. I was hoping that Tyler and Riggs were together and happy, when I rounded a curve in the road and came upon an absolutely amazing sight! The clouds were parting and the sun shone through in magnificent rays. I had the immediate feeling that both of them were there with me saying, "Hey, we are doing okay, and we want you to share in our glory by experiencing this beauty."

I am not traditionally religious; however, I am strongly spiritual and have always found my religion and solace in the beauty of nature. Within the next few moments I encountered a spectacular waterfall. I smiled at the thought of Riggs bounding and playing there. I parked the car, climbed past the other tourists, and scrambled up the hillside next to the falls. Halfway up I left the trail and walked out onto a ledge overlooking the falls. Again I imagined how Tyler and Riggs would have en-

joyed this experience. It was like a scene in a fairyland. I was about to begin photographing when the sky opened again, and first one, then two, then three rainbows beamed across the falls. I could not believe it. Suddenly, two bright white gulls flew onto the ledge near where I stood, and at that moment I knew they were the spirits of Tyler and Riggs. I became warm in spite of the cold, wet morning. It was as if they were saying, "Hey, Bruce, you gave us love and happiness, now we want you to find some peace." These days, when I'm feeling sad or lonely, I drift back to that moment and share peace with the spirits of Tyler and Riggs.

Wayne
1987–2003

We have toys from when Wayne was little until he died of suicide at age sixteen. Late one afternoon nine months after he died, I went into Wayne's room to pack up some of the toys. I began separating them into those to keep as sentimental, some to pass down to his little sister, and the ones we would donate to a local organization. I was sad, but there were a lot of good memories, too.

Then I picked up a box of cards and documents from the funeral, and an envelope fell out. It was Wayne's death certificate. I just held it and cried. I was not feeling strong enough to open it but something really pulled at me to read it again. I sat down on his bed and was crying pretty hard as I read over it. Suddenly the room filled with the smell of Wayne's cologne. I had not smelled it since he'd died. It took me a few minutes to realize what it was. I looked around to see if I had disturbed anything that could cause the smell, but did not see anything. The smell lasted for hours and was only in Wayne's room. All evening, I kept going back into the room to see if the smell had disappeared. Each time it was as strong as when I first noticed it. The next morning it was gone and I have not experienced it again. I feel as if Wayne was with me and letting me know he was there.

Nicholas
1979–2002

Our son, Nicholas Marshall, was warm, smart, and had a sharp sense of humor. He was on state championship teams in baseball and hockey. He had lived and traveled around the world. He had just graduated from college.

On July 5, 2002, Nick put a gun in his mouth and pulled the trigger. Nobody saw this coming. Not me, not his mother (a trained counselor), not Mindy, his longtime girlfriend. Everyone had long assumed Nick and Mindy would be married. His suicide seemed impossible. There are no words to describe the devastation we experienced. It had been a difficult year. I lost my best friend unexpectedly, my wife had a stroke, my mother died, and then, a few months later, my son was dead.

Our only other child, Kim, lived several hundred miles away. Kim was expecting her first child the following October. We were looking forward to the birth for all the obvious reasons. We welcomed a new life in the family, but the excitement of birth was tainted by the trauma of death.

I was at work on October 25 when I got the call from Kim. She was still in the birthing room and was calling to announce her new healthy son. Moments after I hung up the phone, it rang again. It was my wife, Sharon. From her voice, I could tell something was amiss. What else could happen? Choked with emotion, she told me that Mindy had just given birth to Nick's son. This birth seemed just as impossible as Nick's death. We had stayed in contact with Mindy, and although she is a slight person, she never looked pregnant. She never missed a period.

This was as much a shock to her as to us. In the middle of the night, she got up to use the bathroom and delivered her son right there. Her sister washed the infant up in the sink and called EMS. Both mother and child were transported to the hospital and deemed healthy.

Mindy named our new grandson Colin Marshall after our son. Marshall is a family name that has been used for five generations in my family. Mindy and Colin live nearby and we see him or keep him almost every weekend and frequently during the week. It is a true miracle. It is at times a bittersweet experience, but he gives us hope and optimism we had been robbed of by Nick's death. I cannot imagine our lives without him.

David
1977–2000

May is a painful month for me now. It is the month we celebrate Mother's Day, the month of my birthday, and the month my son, David, died by suicide. At first I thought maybe he had killed himself the day before Mother's Day on purpose, and it just crushed me. I learned I was wrong about that.

The following May I became sad and anxious again, and I prayed for just one thing, over and over. One day, out of the blue, Franklin, a young student I knew from the high school my son attended, stopped me on the sidewalk and gave me a huge hug. I was surprised, but it felt good. Nearly every day after that Franklin gave me a hug. I thought this quite strange, but I accepted them because I liked him and they felt so good. One day, after a nice hug from him, I was driving back to work and I began to cry. What I had been praying for all month was a hug from my son for Mother's Day, and it had taken a lot of hugs for me to realize that he was giving me my wish through someone else! I was so happy.

In May of the following year, on my birthday, I was feeling sad again. I work in a day care center, and as I served breakfast to the children, one of the little girls gave me a beautiful rose that she had picked just for me. Her mother said they walked out of the house and this rose was blooming for the first time. Her daughter told her they must have that rose for Mrs. Karen. No one knew it was my birthday, so I knew David had made sure I had a rose. It has helped my grief process so much to know that my son is happy and that he loves me as much as I love him.

Fred
1970–2003

I celebrated Easter of 2003 with my two sons, Mark and Fred, and other members of my family and friends. Two of the children had brought a bag of plastic eggs for adults to hide for them. Mark and a friend hid the eggs a few times so that the children could find them quickly. Then Fred said he would hide the eggs so that they wouldn't be so easy to find. He did so, and it took quite a while to find them. One of the green eggs was never found and remained hidden, since Fred had gone home.

I had no idea that would be my last Easter with Fred. I found him in his home on May 17, dead by suicide.

Two years later, two days before Easter, on my way to my apartment, I was surprised to find a green plastic egg on the grass at the edge of the walkway. It was dirty and scuffed. I picked it up and knew instantly that this was the lost egg that Fred had hidden the month before he died. For me, this was a message from Fred. He was telling me he was all right. The egg is a symbol of new life, and the message to me was that Fred was doing fine in his new life.

The cleaned-up egg now sits next to his picture. It reminds me that he is no longer in any pain and he wants me to know he loves me.

Joshua
1980–2001

The spiritual connections I have felt with my son, Joshua, have helped me more than anything to learn to live with the enormous pain of his suicide. They have strengthened my belief that Josh is okay and at peace. I have agreed to share four of them, with the hope that you will keep yourself open to miracles from your loved one.

The first communication occurred two weeks after Josh's suicide. A friend suggested it would be good for me to get out of town for a day. We drove to a waterfront town several miles away and walked around. It was a beautiful summer day, and as I watched the young couples floating down the river in inner tubes, I couldn't help but think that my son and his fiancée would never enjoy that experience.

The thought made me sad, and I wandered away from my friend and sat at the water's edge. Crying, I took my shoes off and rested my bare feet on a rock. Two mating dragonflies startled me by landing on my big toe. I sat very still and watched them until they flew away. I felt something significant had just happened but I wasn't sure what. I got up and walked a little further downstream and sat down. Again, the pair of dragonflies landed on my toe. This time I paid more attention and I felt this was a message from Josh and his fiancée (it had been a double suicide) that they were together and all right. I felt a much-needed sense of peace.

One night while in bed I had a vision of Josh. I am not sure

I was asleep since it wasn't like a dream. I saw him standing before me, just the two of us in space. I asked him if I could touch him and I asked the question without speaking and he smiled and answered without speaking. I put my arms around him and hugged him and he hugged me. He let me know that he was all right, and then it was over. It was a vivid and powerful encounter, leaving me with a feeling that Josh was in a safe and loving place.

Another instance that was particularly funny happened months later in the fall. By this time I had had numerous communications from Josh, but I was having a bad day, so as I walked through the park, I began talking to Josh. I told him I missed him and that I needed him to let me know he was with me. I needed to feel his presence. I said I was hard headed and if he wanted to get through to me he really had to hit me with it. I am very impatient, and when nothing happened within the first minute or two I felt despondent again. Then, without any warning, a small branch fell from a tree and hit me squarely in the chest! I could almost hear Josh laughing, and I smiled the rest of the way home.

The strongest and most powerful connection came for me on the first anniversary of Josh's death. My family had come to stay with me and when I awoke before the others, I went for my usual walk around the park. On the way back home, I stopped at an art gallery to check out any new paintings by my favorite local artist, who uses wonderfully vibrant colors in landscapes, flowers, and still lifes. The first painting I saw took my breath away. It was a painting of a path through the woods. On the path in the foreground stood an adolescent girl looking away from the viewer and down the path at my son. The young man in the painting wore orange shorts and carried a towel over his shoulder. His facial features, stance, hair color, and body proportions all matched my son's. I was without words. I bought the painting and mentioned that this was the first time I had seen people in paintings done by this particular artist and the shop owner agreed. I asked them to have the artist call me at her convenience. She never called. When I returned home with the painting, I asked my daughter where she thought I should hang it. She gasped and asked me if that was Josh. My parents also thought it was Josh. Later that night a friend of mine visited, and when he saw the painting he asked me when I had commissioned it. There is absolutely no doubt that the young man is my son. I even have the orange shorts among his clothes that I cannot part with.

A question arose about the girl in the painting. She looks nothing like Josh's fiancée. My immediate reaction upon seeing the painting was that it was me as a younger woman, and a close friend of mine verified that. That part of the message remains my secret. When I look at the painting, I hear my son telling me that he will lead me, that I should trust him. He reminds me that I am a spiritual being in a physical world and that I should have faith in God, that all is as it should be. I am on a spiritual path and if I follow that path everything will be all right.

I finally met the artist at one of her showings and I asked about my picture. At first she said she didn't know what made her put figures in that one painting, but when I told her who the boy was, she cried. As we hugged each other, she told me that a vision of that boy had come to her in a dream one night. About a year ago.

Notes

Chapter One

1. American Association of Suicidology, "U.S.A. Suicide: 2002 Official Data," http://www.suicidology.org/associations/1045/files/2002FinalData.pdf.

2. Christopher Lucas and Henry Seiden, *Silent Grief: Living in the Wake of Suicide* (Northvale, NJ: Jason Aronson, 1987), 5.

3. American Foundation for Suicide Prevention, "Facts about Suicide: Firearms and Suicide," http://www.afsp.org/index-1.htm.

4. Suicide Awareness Voices of Education, "Facts about Suicide in United States," http://www.save.org/basics/facts.html.

5. World Health Organization, "Address on World Violence Report," http://www.who.int/dg/lee/speeches/2004/puerto_ordaz_violencereport/en/.

6. American Association of Suicidology, "U.S.A. Suicide: 2002 Official Data," http://www.suicidology.org/associations/1045/files/2002FinalData.pdf, and American Foundation for Suicide Prevention, "About Youth Suicide," http://www.afsp.org/index-1.htm.

7. Light for Life Foundation, "Yellow Ribbon Suicide Prevention Program," http://www.yellowribbonsd.org/.

8. World Health Organization, "Figures and Facts about Suicide," http://www.who.int/mental_health/media/en/382.pdf.

9. Edwin S. Shneidman, interview by the authors, August 21, 2004, Los Angeles.

10. American Association of Suicidology, "U.S.A. Suicide: 2002 Official Data," http://www.suicidology.org/associations/1045/files/2002FinalData.pdf and YouthSuicide.pdf.

11. World Health Organization, "Figures and Facts about Suicide," http://www.who.int/mental_health/media/en/382.pdf.

Chapter Two

1. Edwin S. Shneidman, *The Suicidal Mind* (New York: Oxford University Press, 1996), 25.

2. Ibid., 4.

3. Edwin S. Shneidman, interview by the authors, August 20, 2004, Los Angeles.

Chapter Three

1. Kay Redfield Jamison, *Night Falls Fast: Understanding Suicide* (New York: Alfred A. Knopf, 1999), 31.

Chapter Five

1. Gary Burnett, director, Critical Incidence Response Program, interview by Jean Larch, May 20, 2005, Chesterfield, Michigan.

2. Dr. Patricia Yoder, interview by Jean Larch, October 23, 2004, Clinton Township, Michigan.

3. Dennis Liegghio, survivor and musician, interview by Jean Larch, June 13, 2005, Clinton Township, Michigan.

Chapter Six

1. Edwin S. Shneidman, Norman Farberow, and Robert E. Litman, *The Psychology of Suicide: A Clinician's Guide to Evaluation and Treatment* (Northvale, NJ: Jason Aronson, 1994), 91–92.

Information adapted from works of Edwin S. Shneidman, Ph.D., a founder of the field of suicidology and of the American Association of Suicidology, is used with permission and was obtained through interviews by the authors, August 20 and 21, 2004, Los Angeles; and telephone interviews by Jean Larch, September 24, November 14, and December 7, 2004.

Resources

Authors' Web Site

Contact Jean Larch and Beverly Cobain at www.livingmatters.com.

Crisis Centers and Hotlines

Kristin Brooks Hope Center
http://hopeline.com
1-800-SUICIDE (1-800-784-2433)

National Suicide Prevention Lifeline
www.suicidepreventionlifeline.org
1-800-273-TALK (1-800-273-8255)
24 hours a day, 7 days a week

Survivors of Suicide Support Groups

American Association of Suicidology Support Group Directory: http://www.suicidology.org/associations/1045/files/Support_Groups.cfm

Other Web Site Resources

American Association of Suicidology (AAS): www.suicidology.org

American Foundation for Suicide Prevention (AFSP): www.afsp.org

Centers for Disease Control and Prevention (CDC): www.cdc.gov

Facts and Fables on Suicide:
http://members.aol.com/MikeRickrd/suicidefactsnfables.html

National Alliance for the Mentally Ill (NAMI):
www.nami.org

National Center for Health Statistics (NCHS):
www.cdc.gov/nchs

Suicide Awareness Voices of Education (SAVE):
www.save.org

Suicide Prevention Action Network USA (SPAN):
www.spanusa.org

World Health Organization (WHO): www.who.int

Yellow Ribbon Suicide Prevention Program (YRSPP)
"Light for Life": www.yellowribbonsd.org

Alternative Therapies for Emotional Trauma

EMDR Institute: www.emdr.com
Comprehensive information about Eye Movement Desensitization and Reprocessing as a therapy for trauma disorders.

Tapas Acupressure Technique: www.tat-intl.com
"Unstress for Success" site describes this effective process and offers free instructions to help with trauma relief.

Emotional Freedom Techniques: www.emofree.com
This site discusses the basics of Energy Psychology and offers a provider directory.

Publications

Hay, Louise L. *You Can Heal Your Life*. Santa Monica, California: Hay House, 1984.

Lucas, Christopher, and Henry Seiden. *Silent Grief: Living in the Wake of Suicide*. Northvale, New Jersey: Jason Aronson, 1987.

Rothschild, Joel. *Signals*. Novato, California: New World Library, 2000.

Shapiro, Francine, and Margot Silk Forrest. *EMDR: The Breakthrough Therapy for Overcoming Anxiety, Stress, and Trauma*. New York: Basic Books, 1997.

Shneidman, Edwin S. *The Suicidal Mind*. New York: Oxford Press, 1996.

Shneidman, Edwin S., and Norman Farberow. *Facts and Fables about Suicide*, PHS Publication 852, U.S. Government Office, 1961.

Shneidman, Edwin S., Norman Farberow, and Robert Litman. *The Psychology of Suicide*. Northvale, New Jersey: Jason Aronson, 1994.

"Suicide and Psychache," *Journal of Nervous and Mental Disease*, 1993, Vol. 181 (147–149).

Tolle, Eckhart. *Power of the Now*. Novato, California: New World Library, 1997.

Index

About the Authors

Beverly Cobain is a registered nurse with certification in psychiatric/mental health nursing. She is a survivor of three family suicides, including that of Kurt Cobain, the lead singer of the band Nirvana, who killed himself in 1994. Kurt's death led Bev to write the acclaimed book *When Nothing Matters Anymore: A Survival Guide for Depressed Teens* and to become a national speaker on the topics of depression and suicide. Bev resides in Costa Rica with her German shepherd, Tosh. She can be reached by e-mail at bevcobain@livingmatters.com.

Jean Larch, SWT, has followed her passion for the past two decades at Macomb County Crisis Center in Chesterfield, Michigan, as a crisis intervention specialist working closely with suicidal individuals and family members who have survived the loss of a loved one due to suicide. She has developed an acclaimed workshop on the subject of the suicidal mind, which continues to benefit both survivors and professionals. She trains mental health professionals on various aspects of suicide. Jean lives with her husband, Mark, in Michigan, near their three children, Sarah, Nate, and Drew.

Beverly Cobain and Jean Larch can both be reached at their Web site, www.livingmatters.com.

Hazelden Publishing and Educational Services is a division of the Hazelden Foundation, a not-for-profit organization. Since 1949, Hazelden has been a leader in promoting the dignity and treatment of people afflicted with the disease of chemical dependency.

The mission of the foundation is to improve the quality of life for individuals, families, and communities by providing a national continuum of information, education, and recovery services that are widely accessible; to advance the field through research and training; and to improve our quality and effectiveness through continuous improvement and innovation.

Stemming from that, the mission of the publishing division is to provide quality information and support to people wherever they may be in their personal journey—from education and early intervention, through treatment and recovery, to personal and spiritual growth.

Although our treatment programs do not necessarily use everything Hazelden publishes, our bibliotherapeutic materials support our mission and the Twelve Step philosophy upon which it is based. We encourage your comments and feedback.

The headquarters of the Hazelden Foundation are in Center City, Minnesota. Additional treatment facilities are located in Chicago, Illinois; New York, New York; Plymouth, Minnesota; and St. Paul, Minnesota. At these sites, we provide a continuum of care for men and women of all ages. Our Plymouth facility is designed specifically for youth and families.

For more information on Hazelden, please call **1-800-257-7800**. Or you may access our World Wide Web site on the Internet at **www.hazelden.org**.